THE JOY OF BELLY DANCE
COLORING BOOK

by Jennifer R. Richardson

I0462663

About the Artist and this Book

Jennifer Richardson is a self-taught artist who has been drawing since she was a child. She enjoys working with various media from graphite to watercolors to ink. She took her first belly dance class in 2013 and has been falling in love with the art form ever since. She wanted to create something to join her love of drawing and her love for the dance and that's how this coloring book came to life.

Belly dance features a rich array of styles and types of dances, many that will be found in The Joy of Belly Dance, including Egyptian Raqs Sharqi, American Cabaret, Raqs al Assaya, Folkloric, and more! The 35 unique illustrations featured in this book are drawn from real belly dancers.

Much appreciation to the dancers who provided photo references for this book:

Asteria Ramona
Cassandra al Warda
Christina Brown
DeLeslyn Brumfield
Elianae
Ellie Akins
Fireflower
Helia
Melika
Melissa Gamal
Nada el Masriya
Raluca Ghiban
Sahara
Vanessa of Cairo
Zaina Brown

ISBN: 9781074060411

Art of Jen

WWW.ART-OF-JEN.COM

INSTAGRAM @ART.OF.JEN

WWW.FACEBOOK.COM/ARTOFJEN

Disclaimer: This book is not created for use with heavy media like watercolors or other paints, use at your own discretion.

Tip: Place a blank sheet of paper under the page you're coloring to prevent bleed onto subsequent pages.

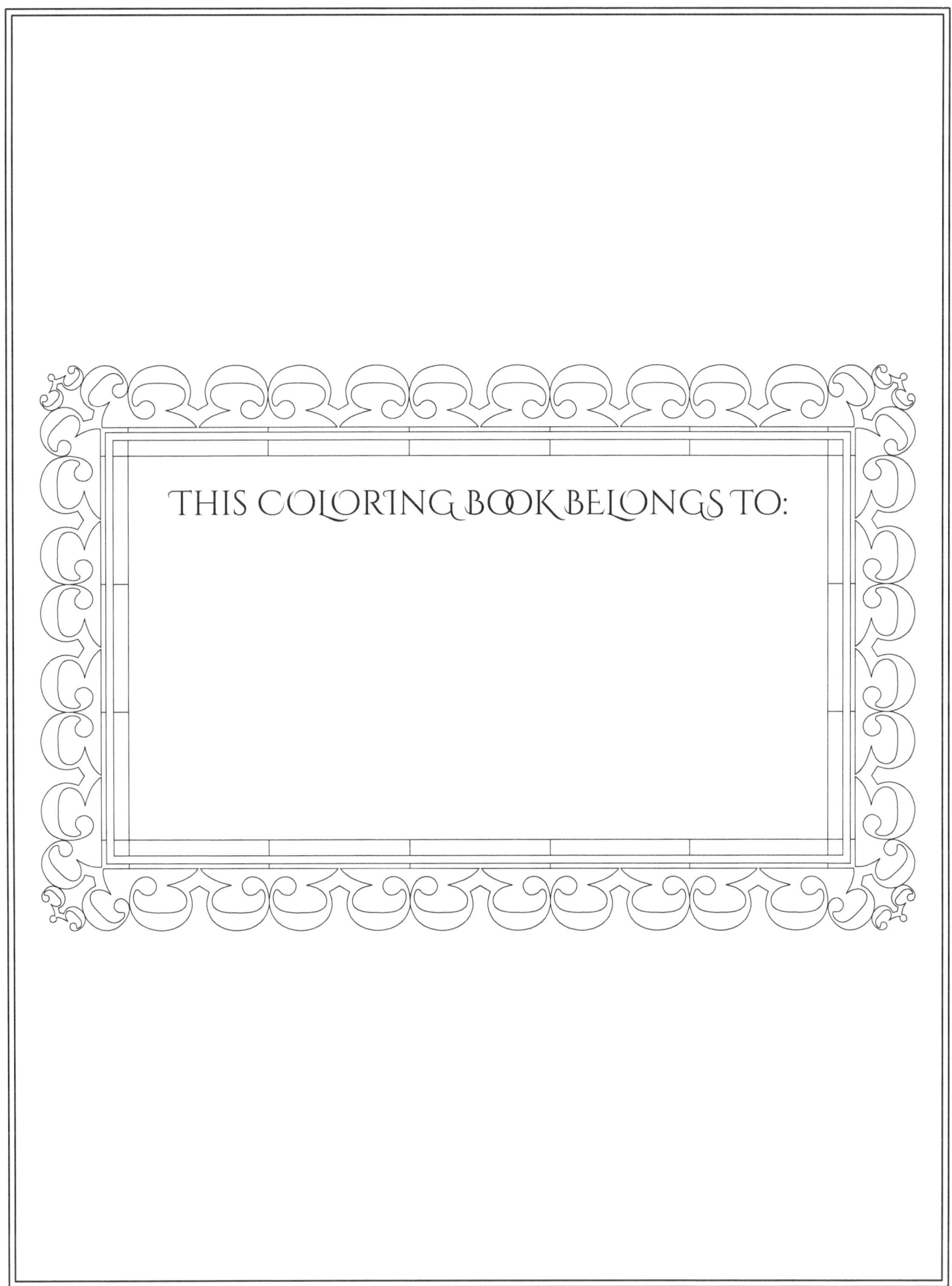

THIS COLORING BOOK BELONGS TO:

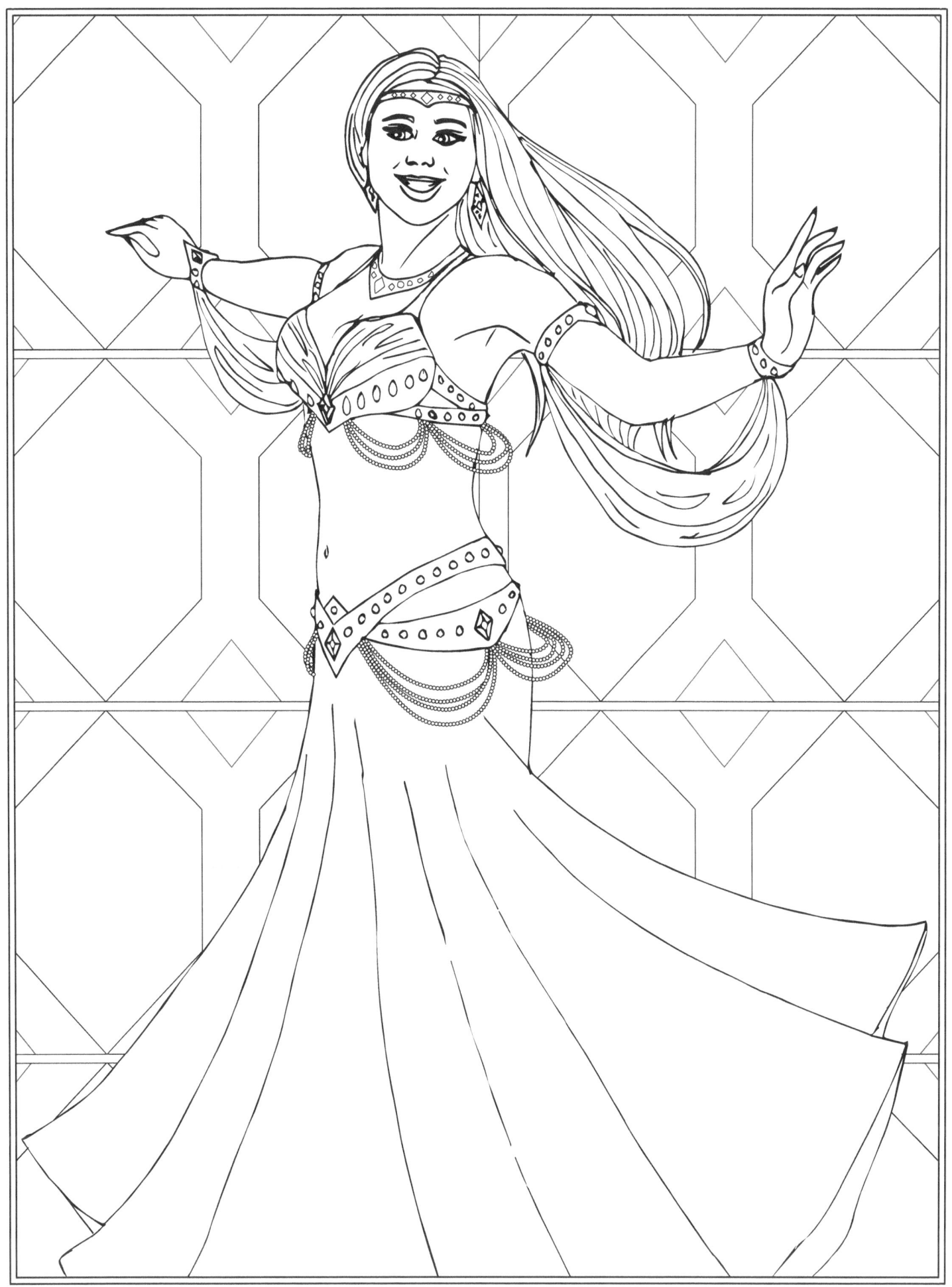

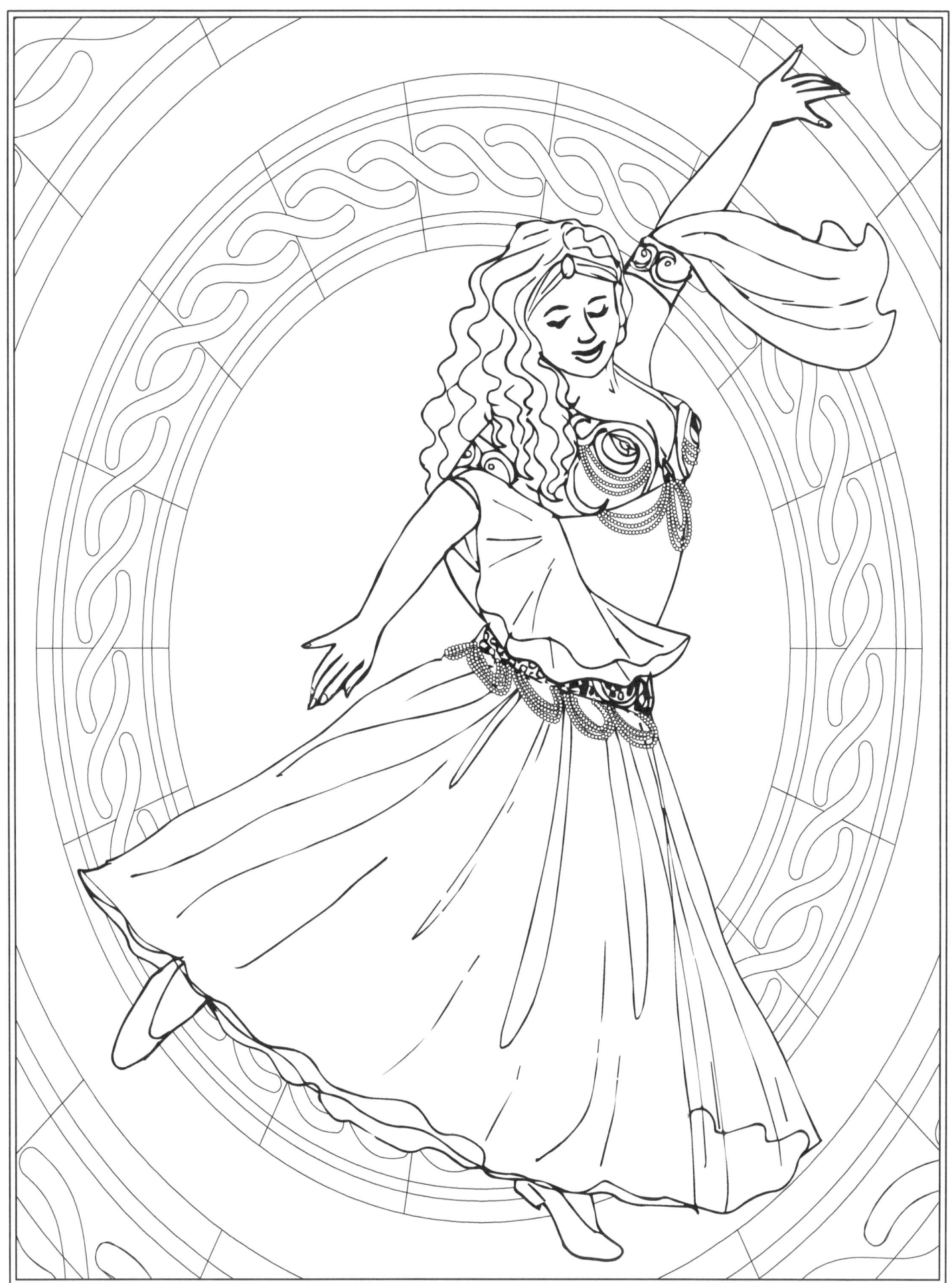

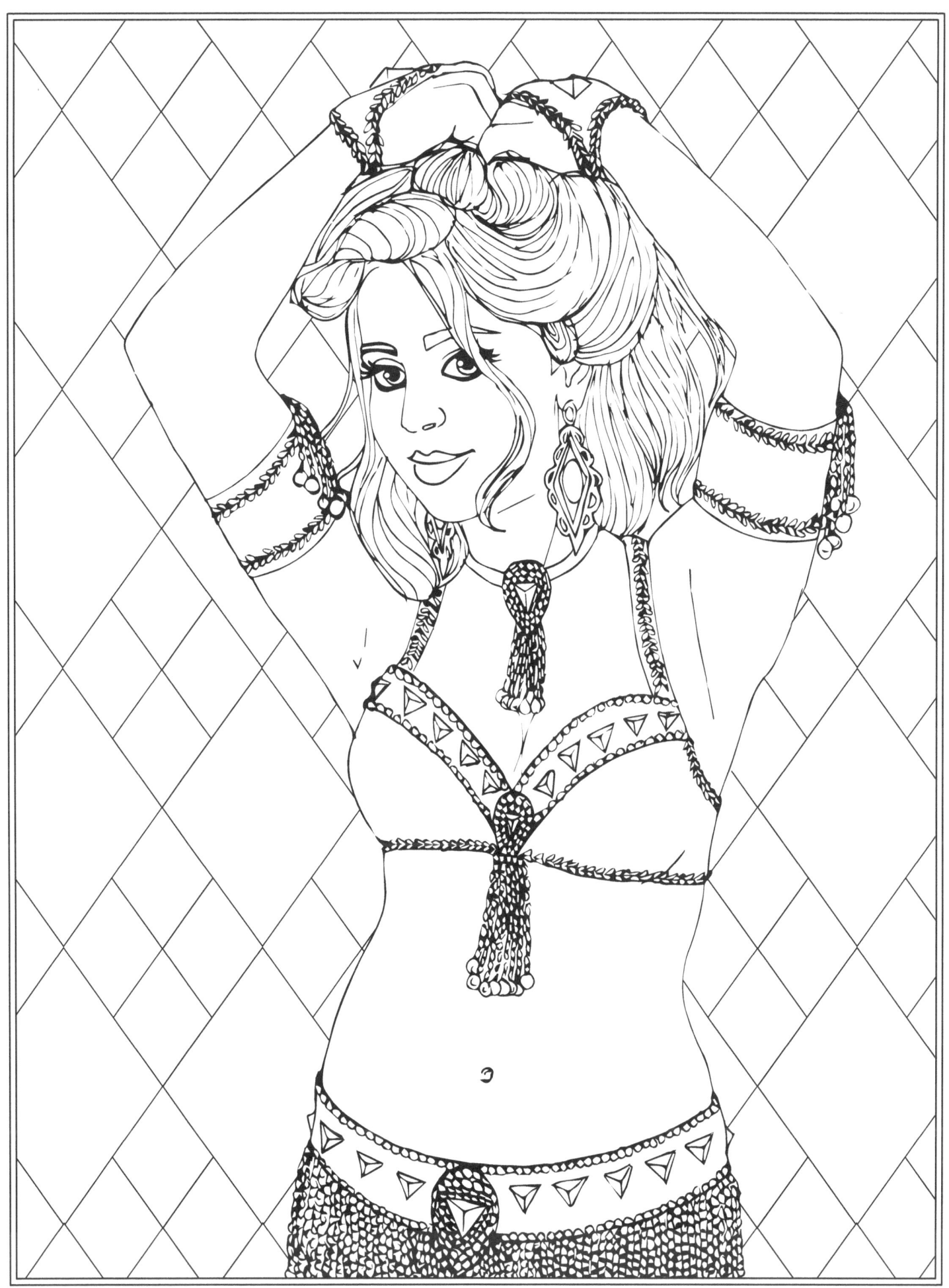

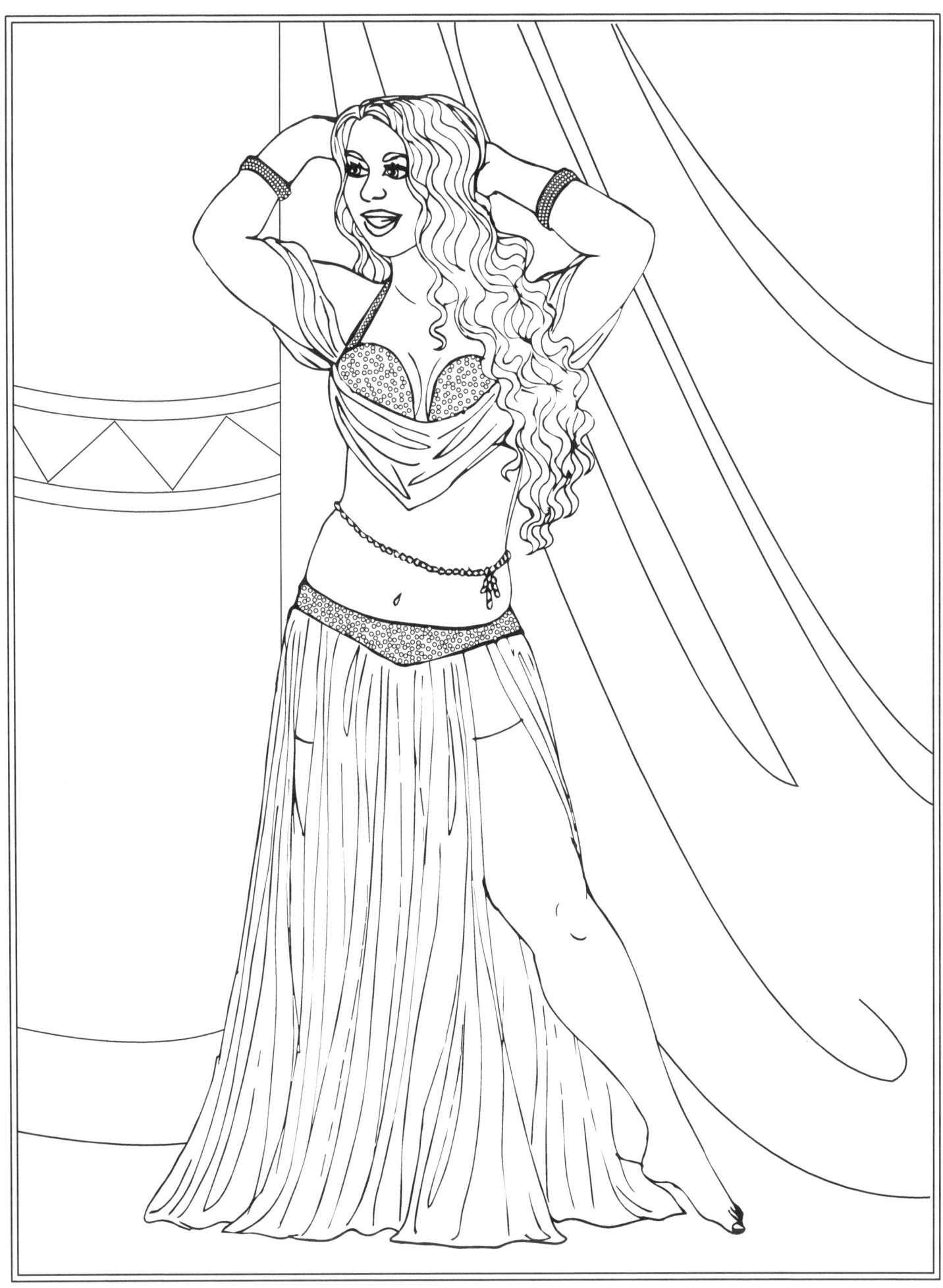

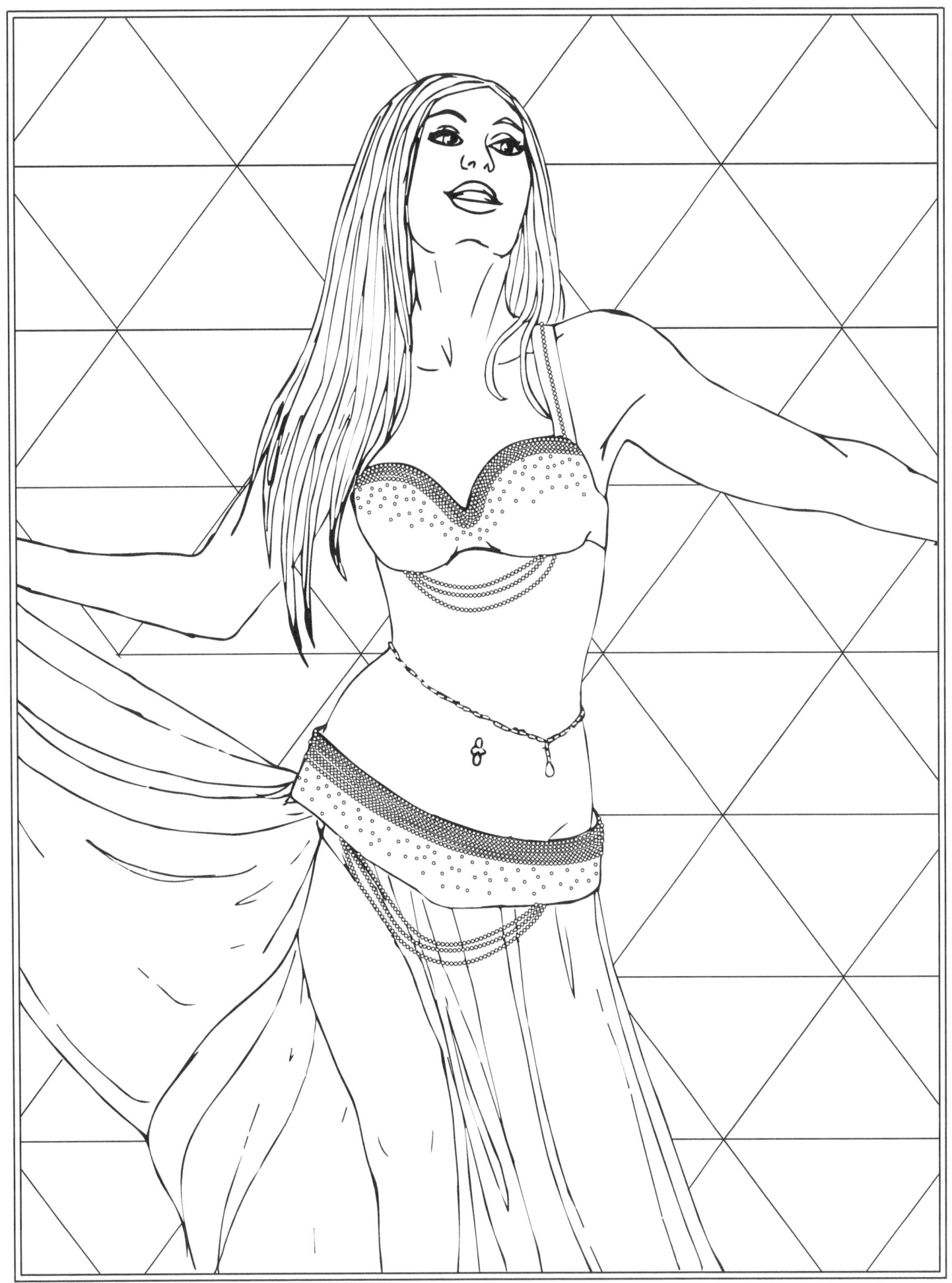

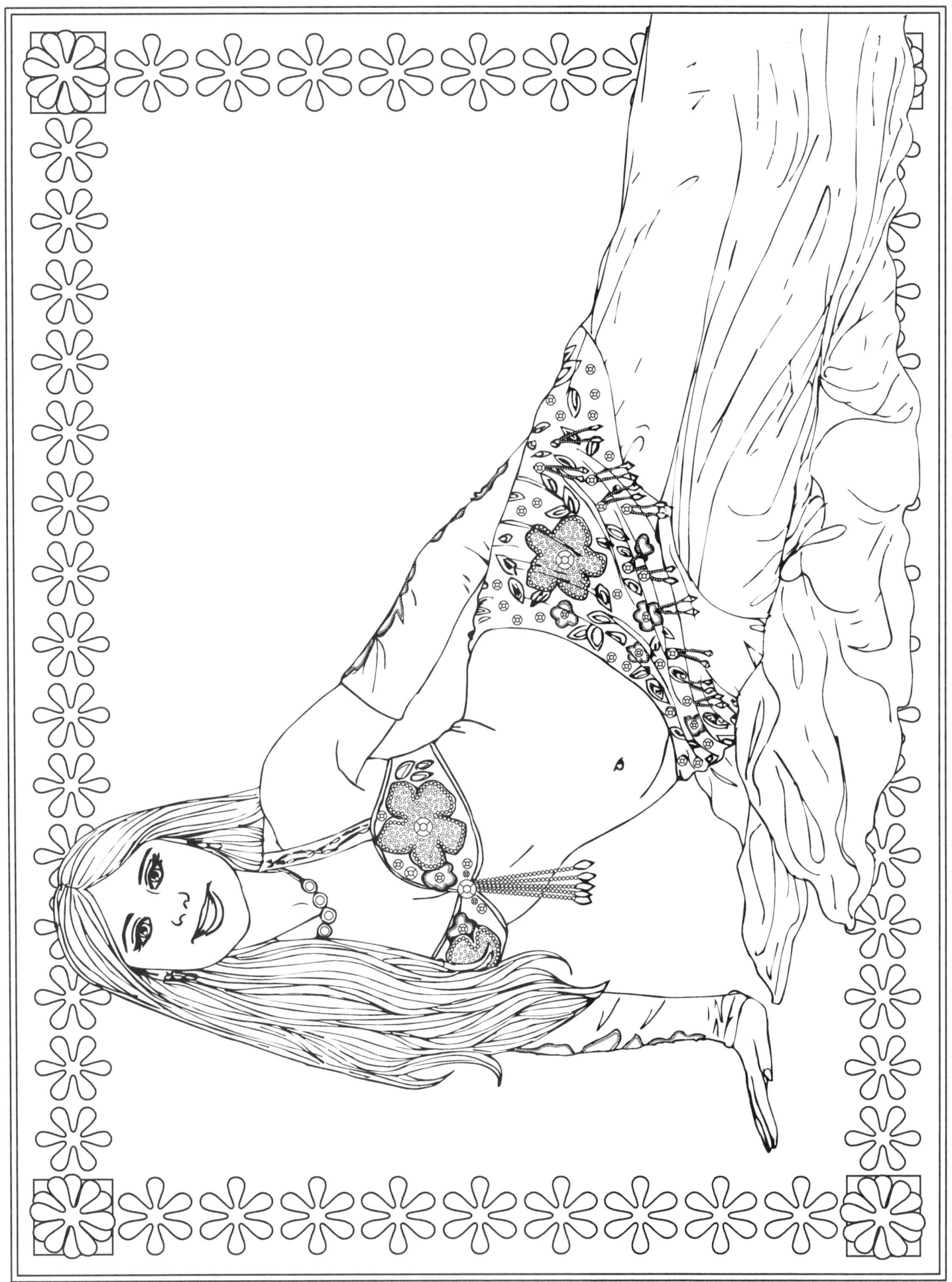

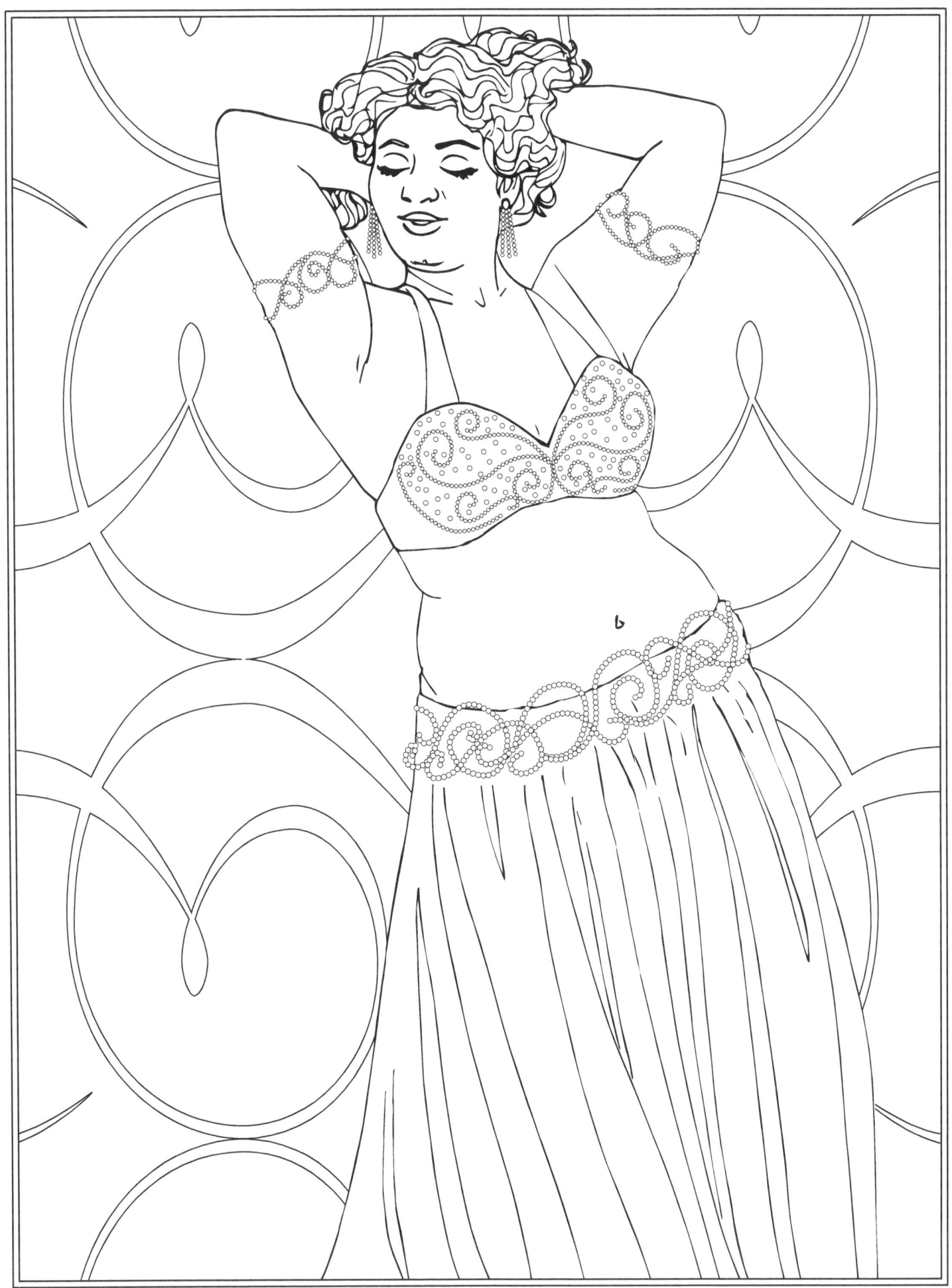

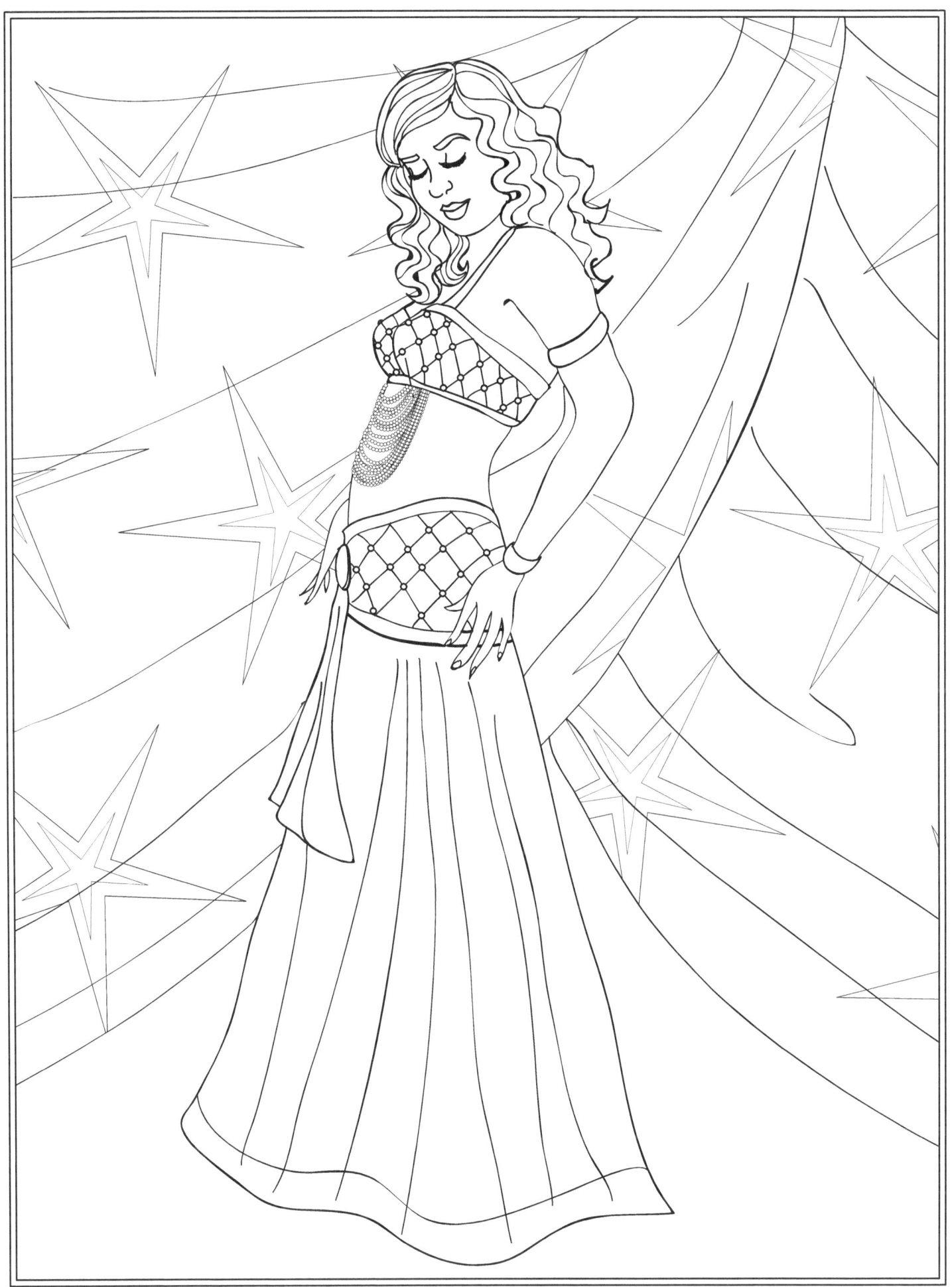

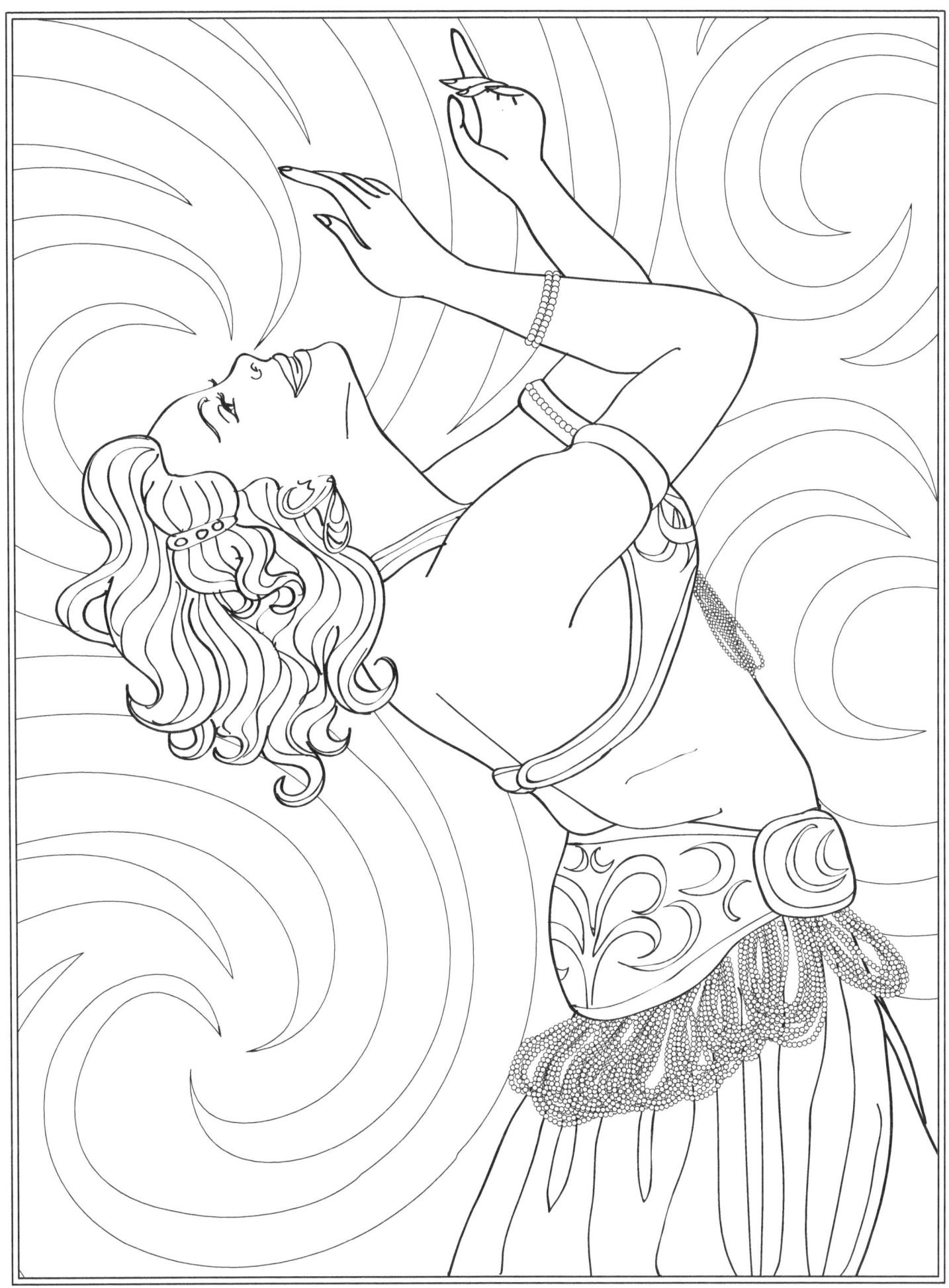

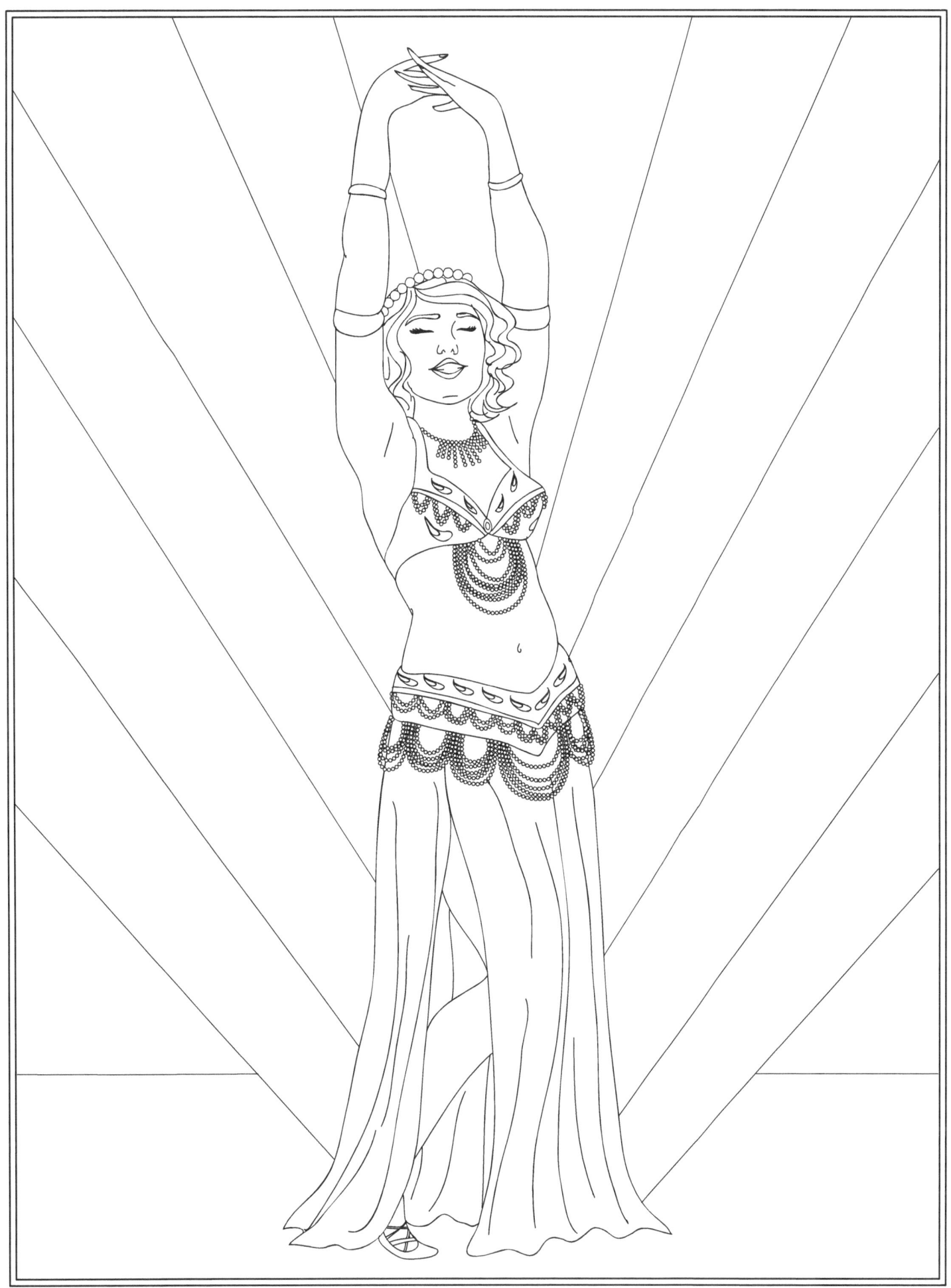

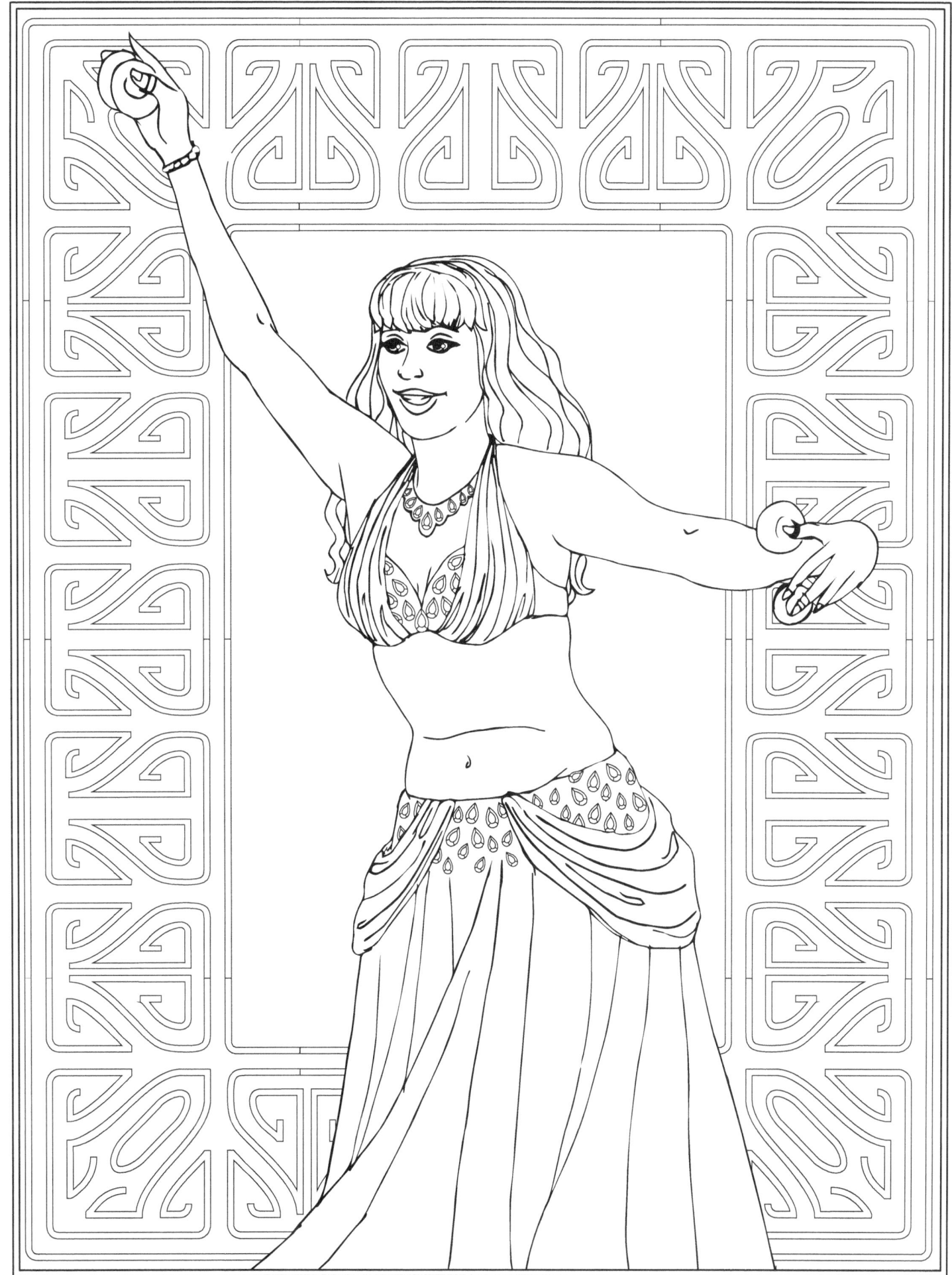

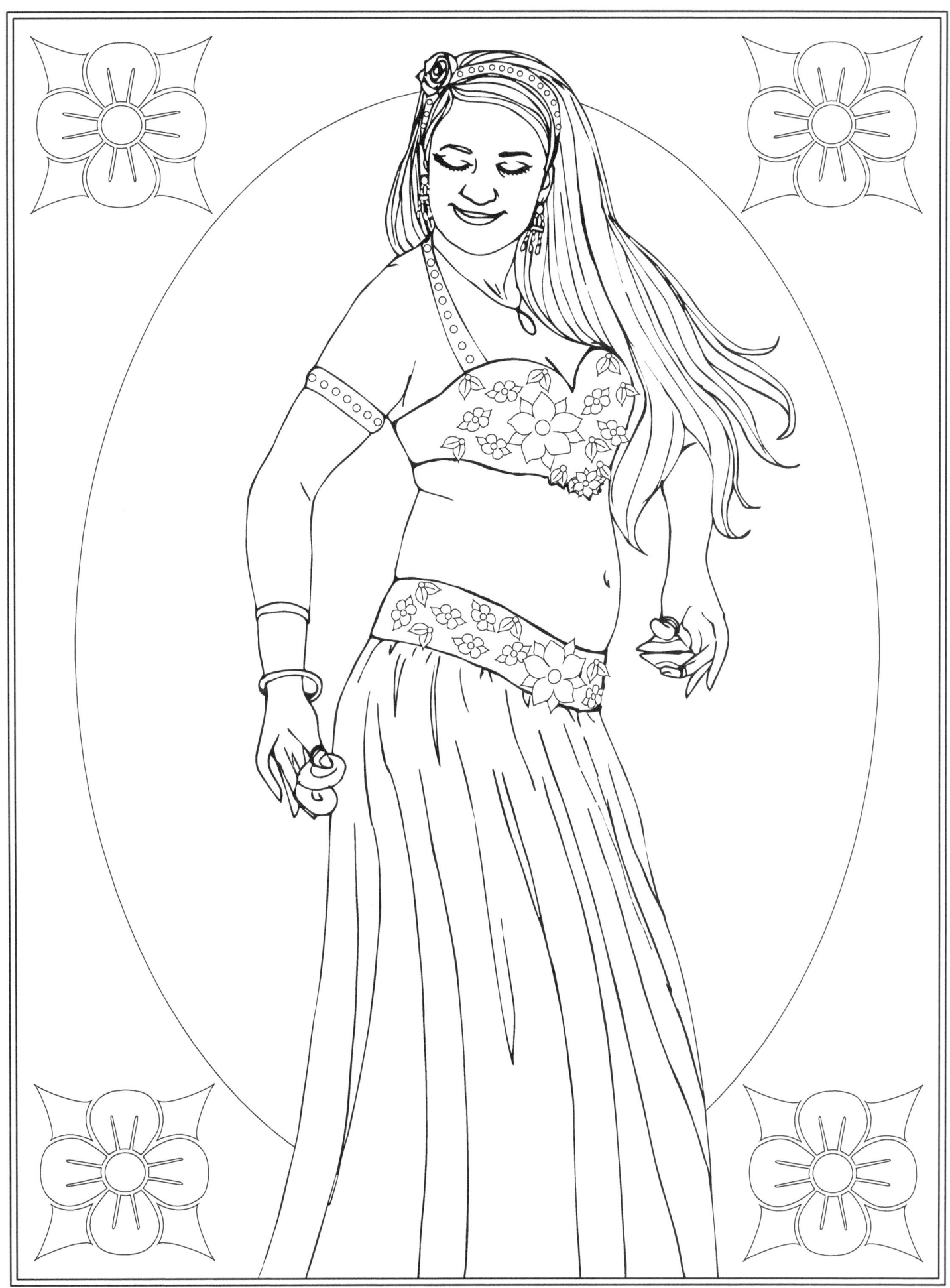

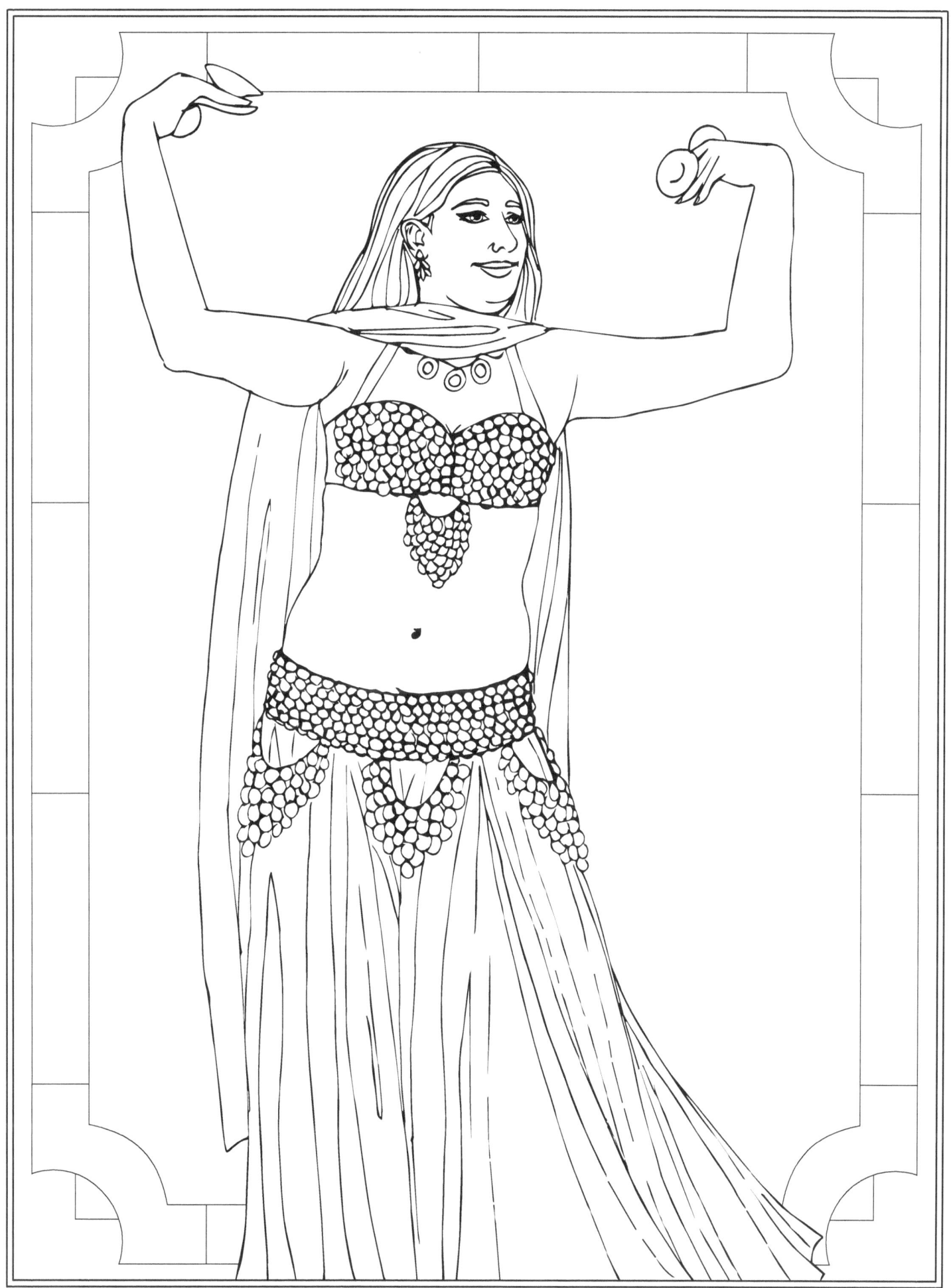

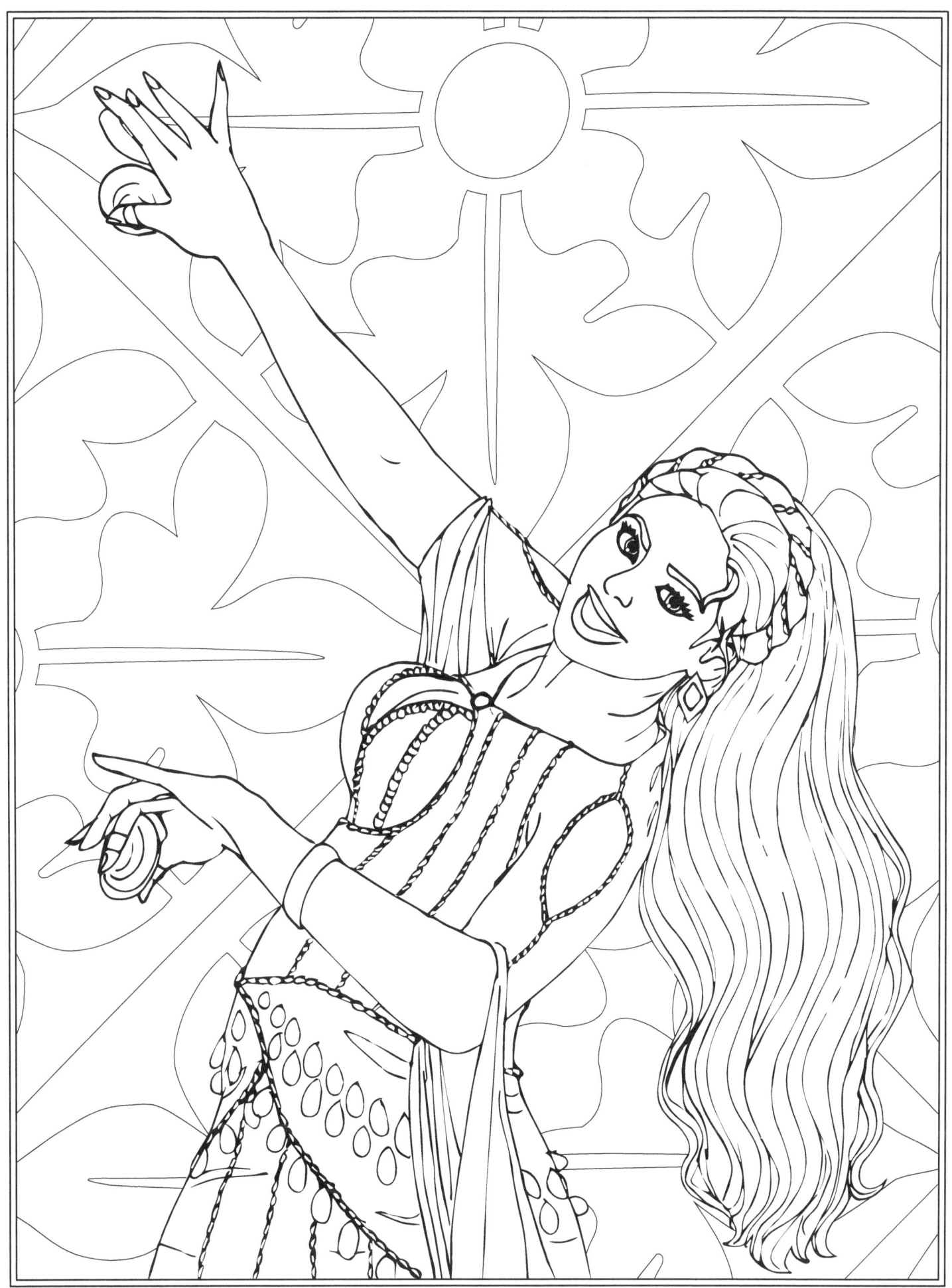

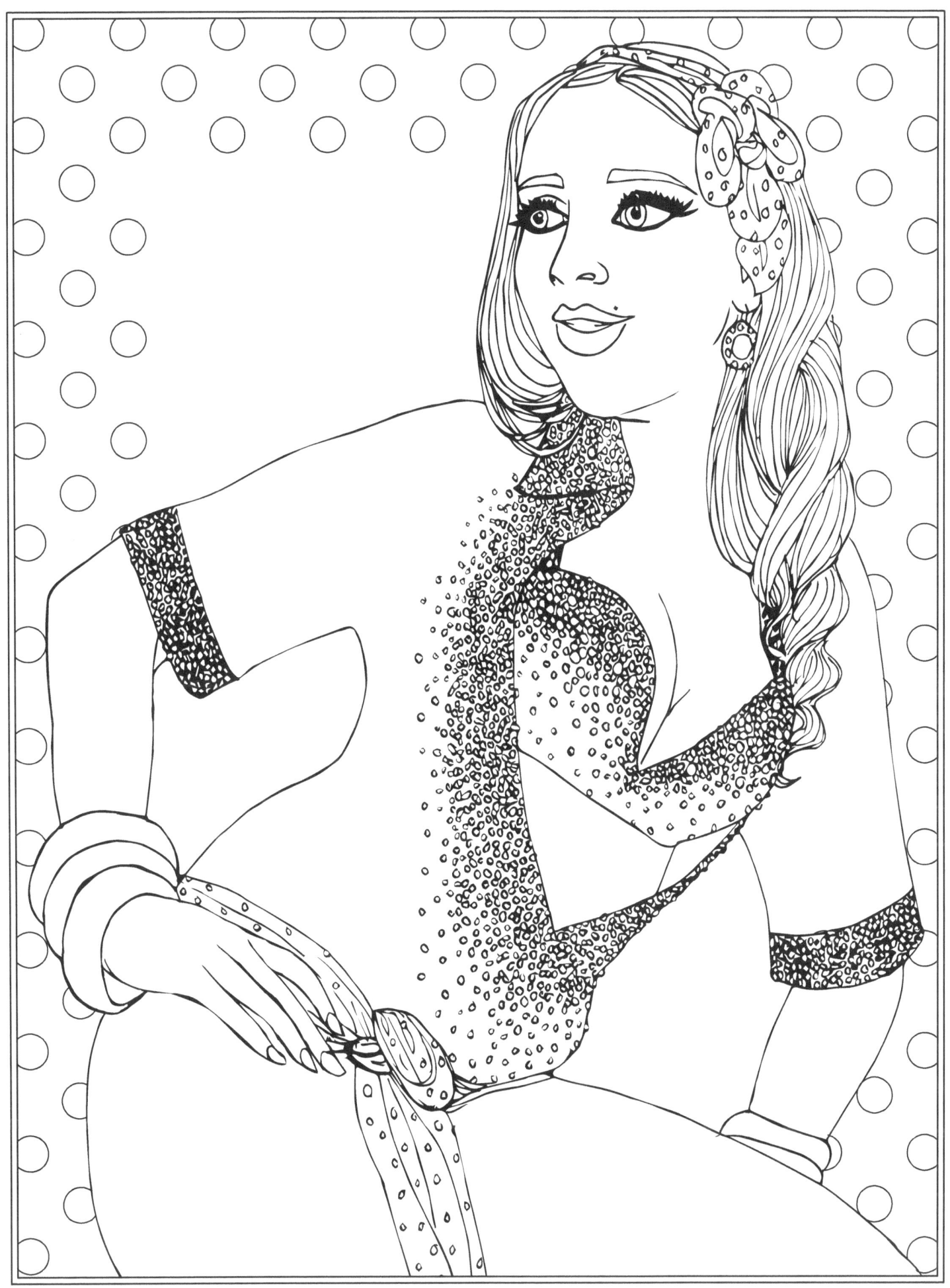

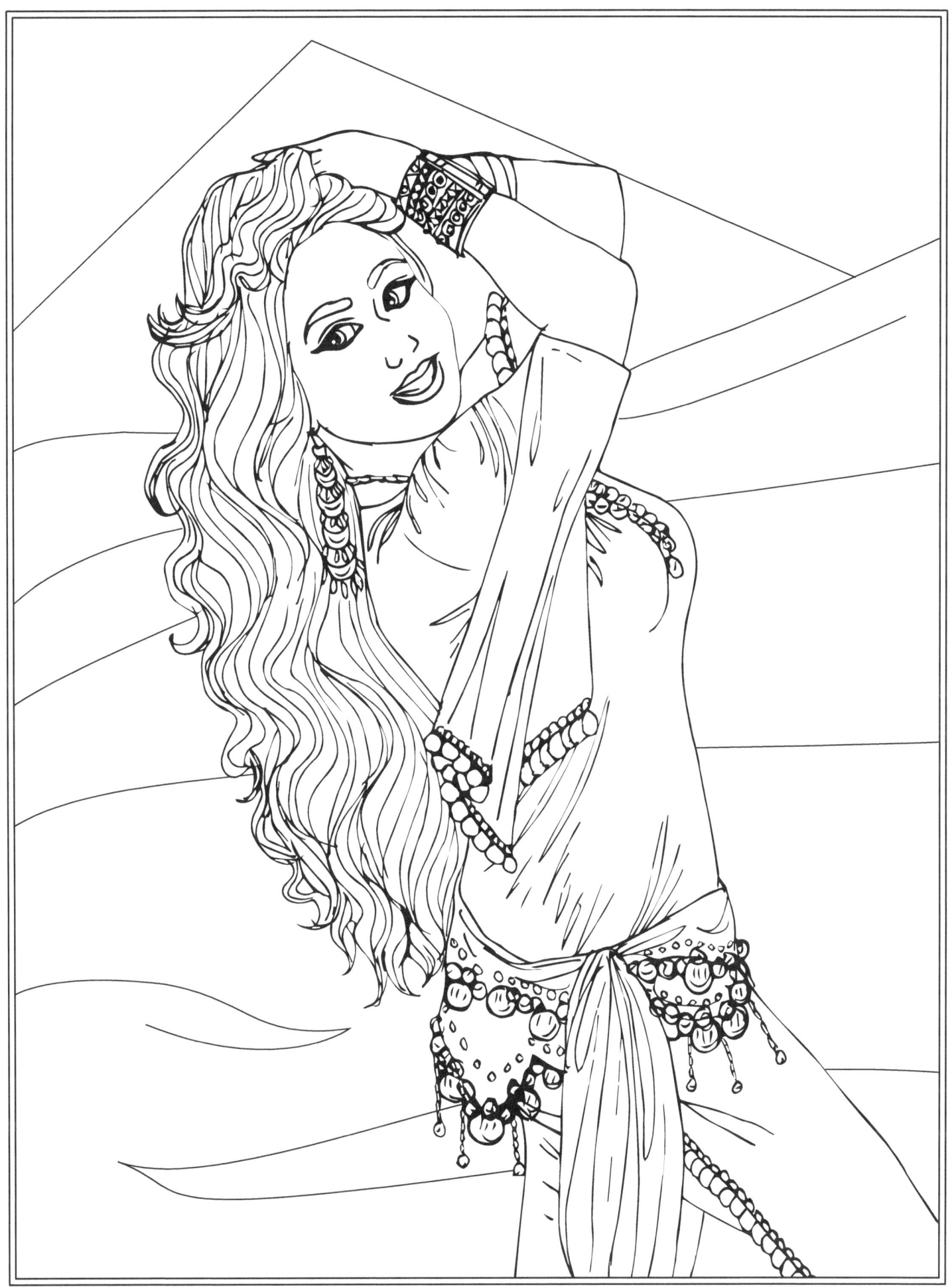

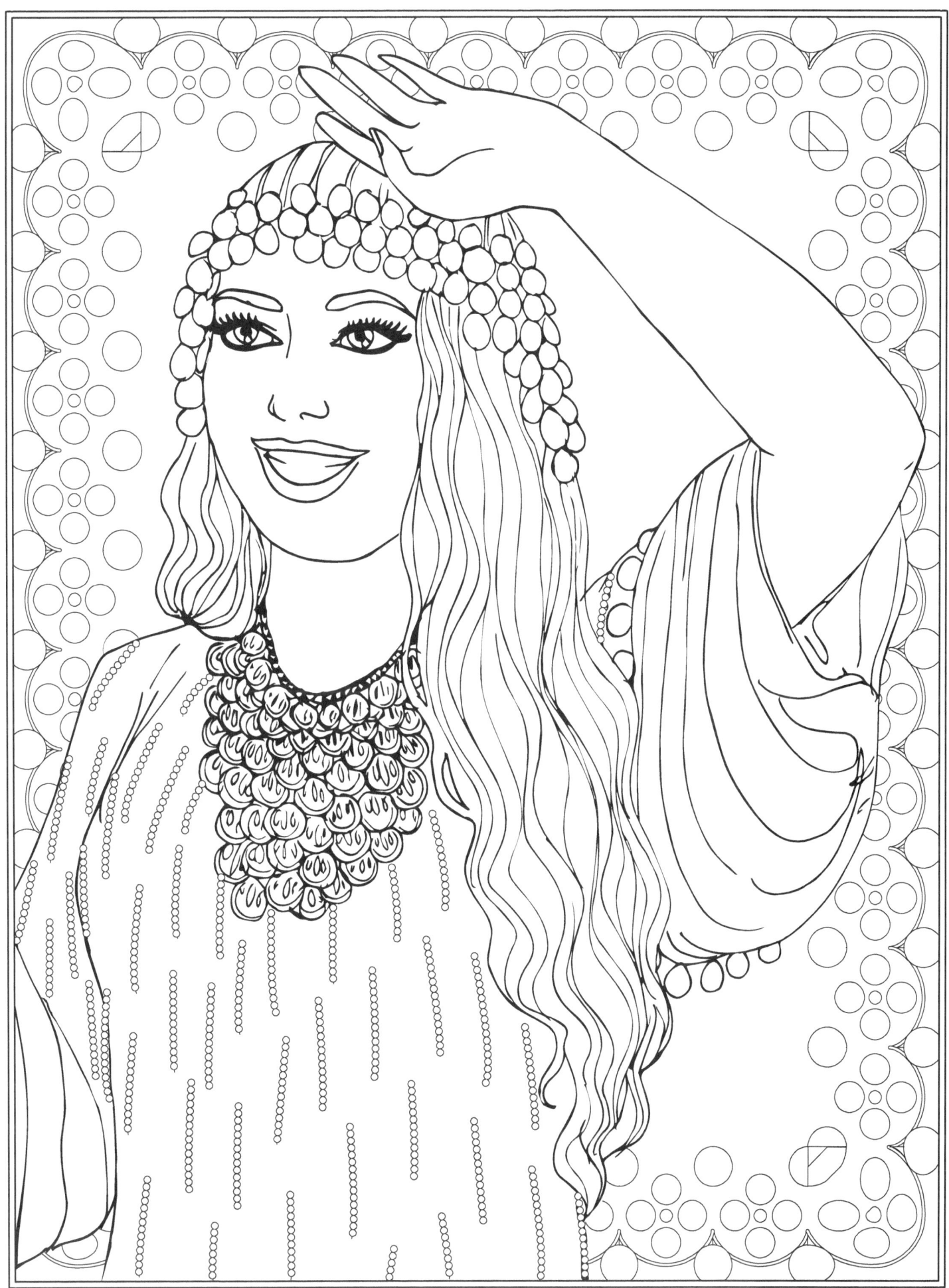

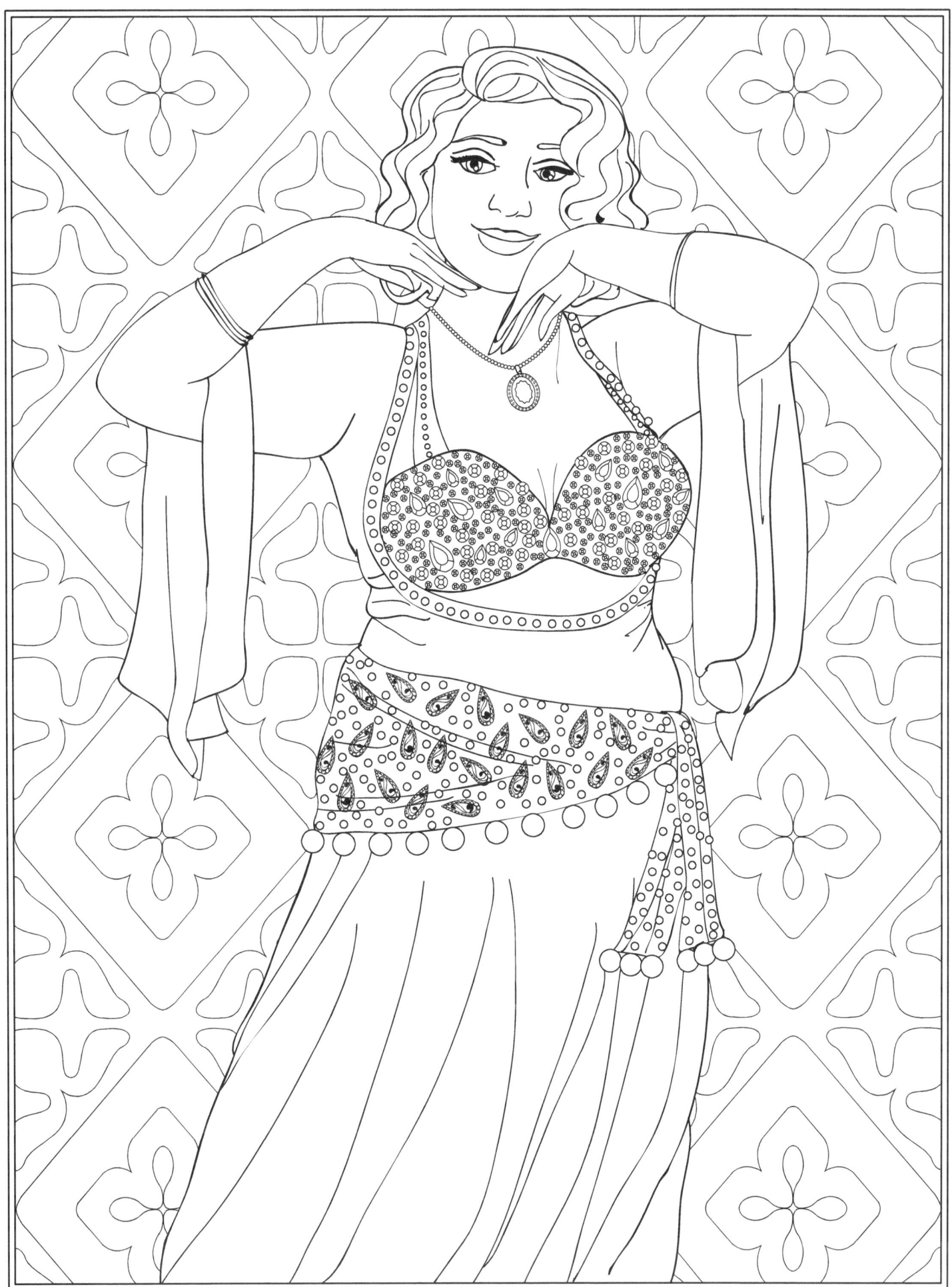

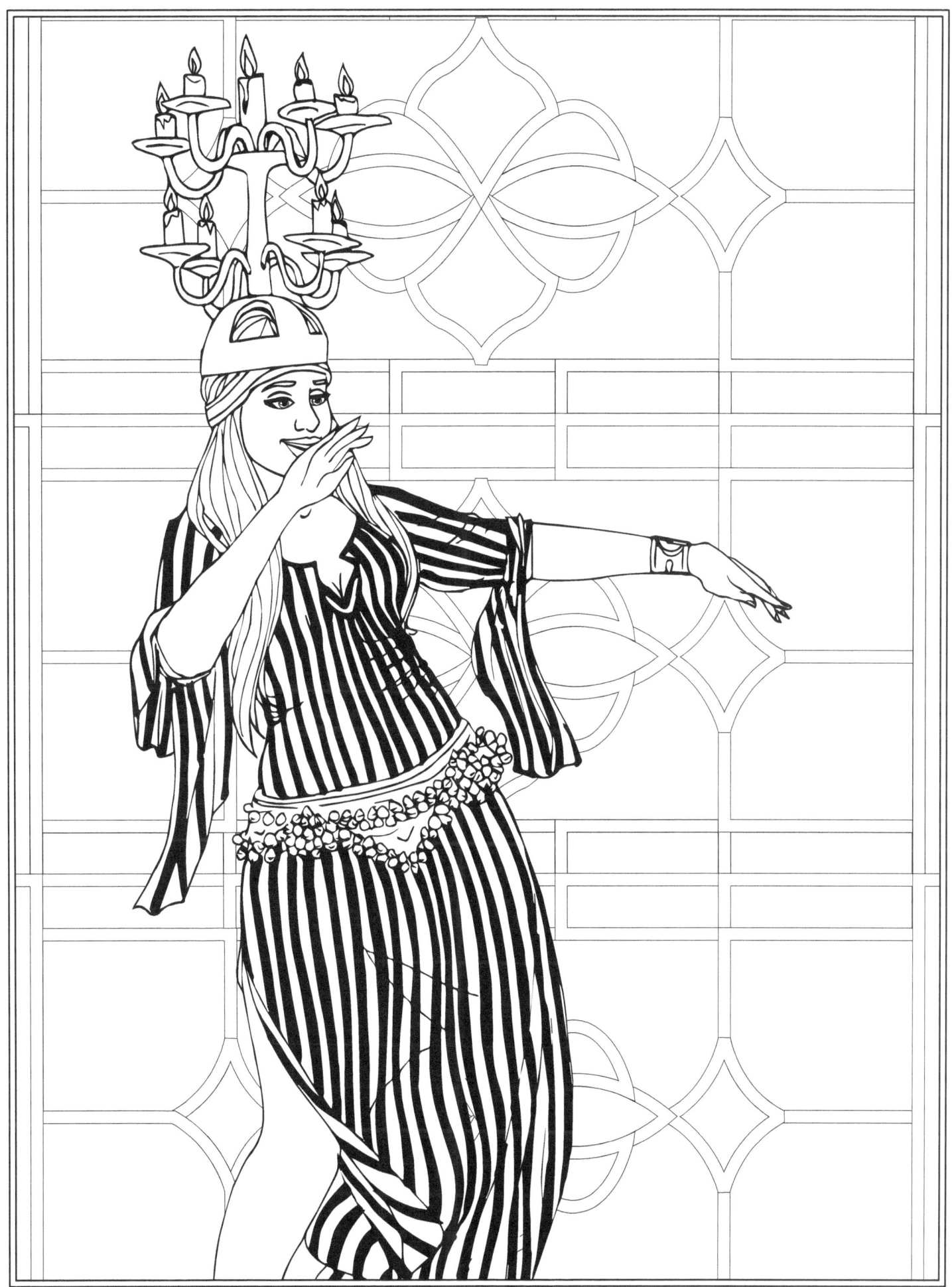

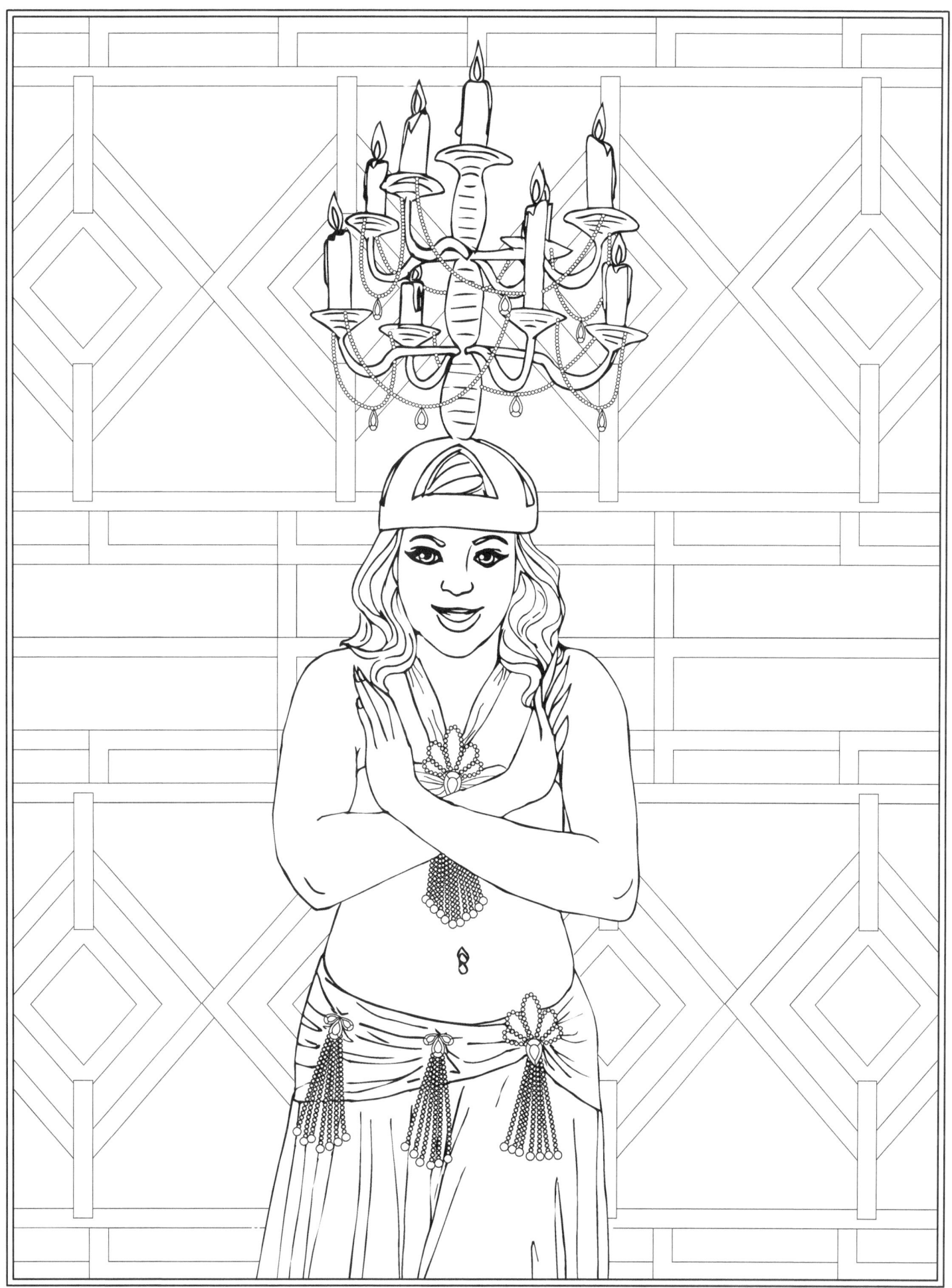

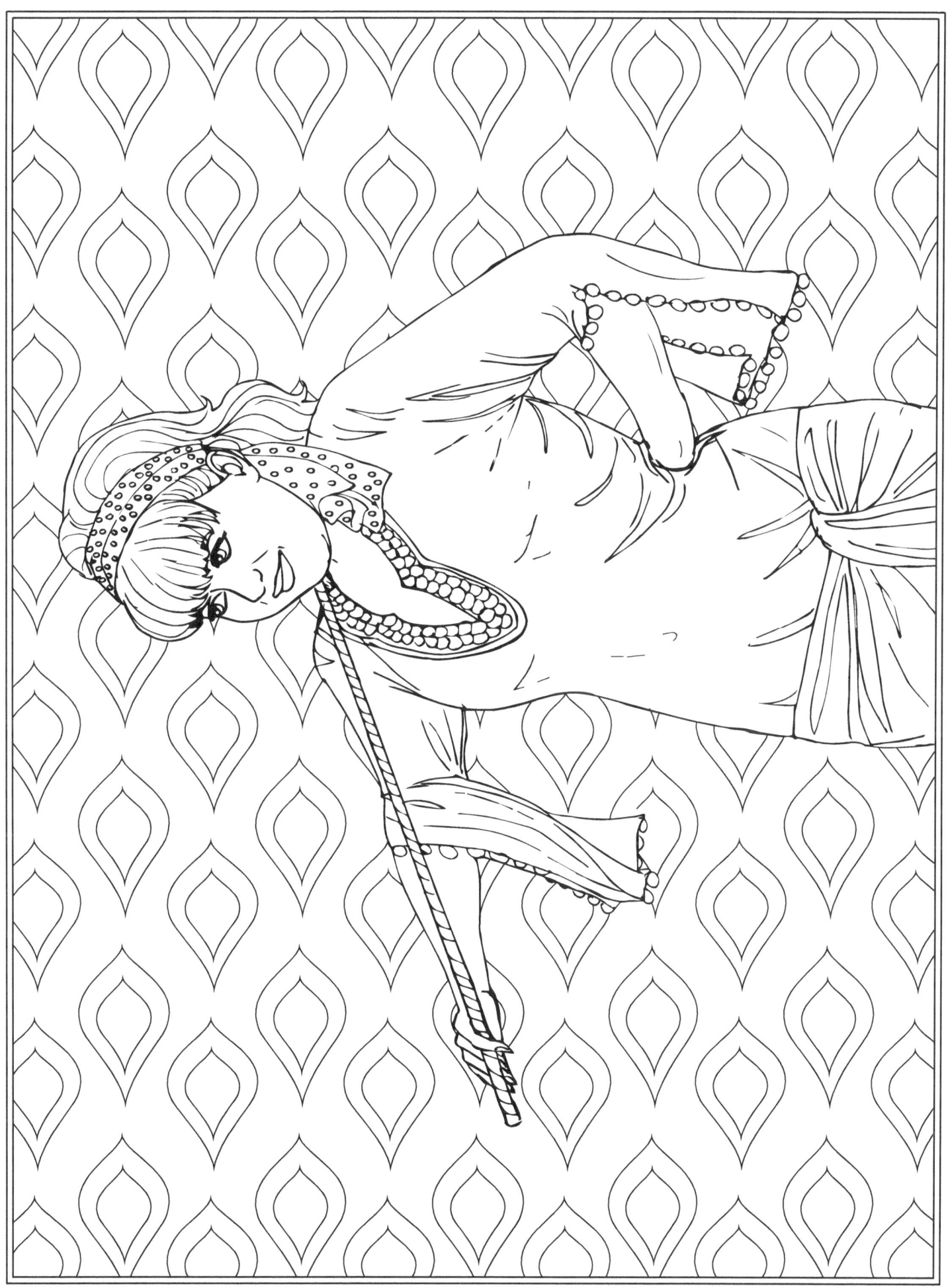

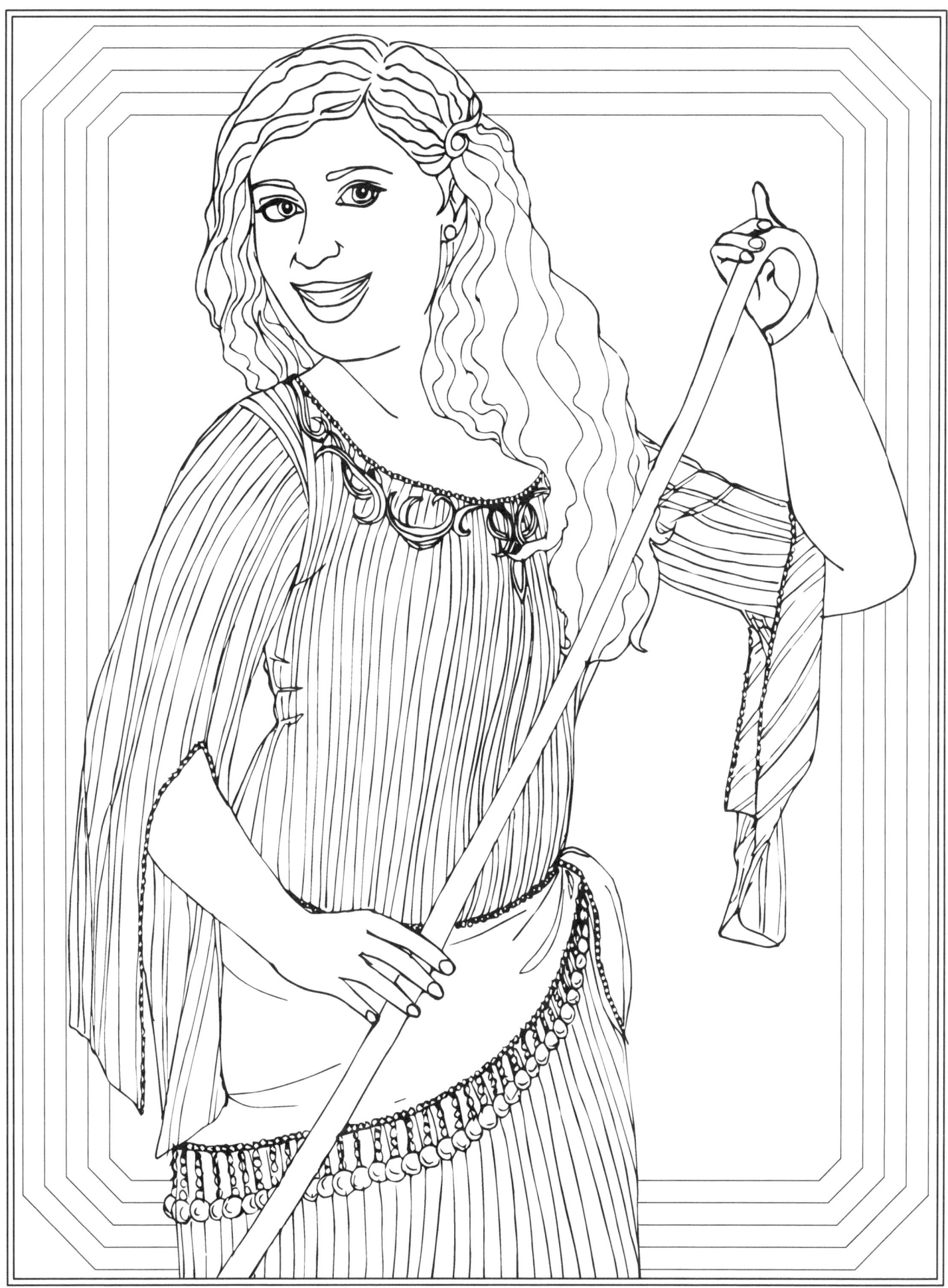

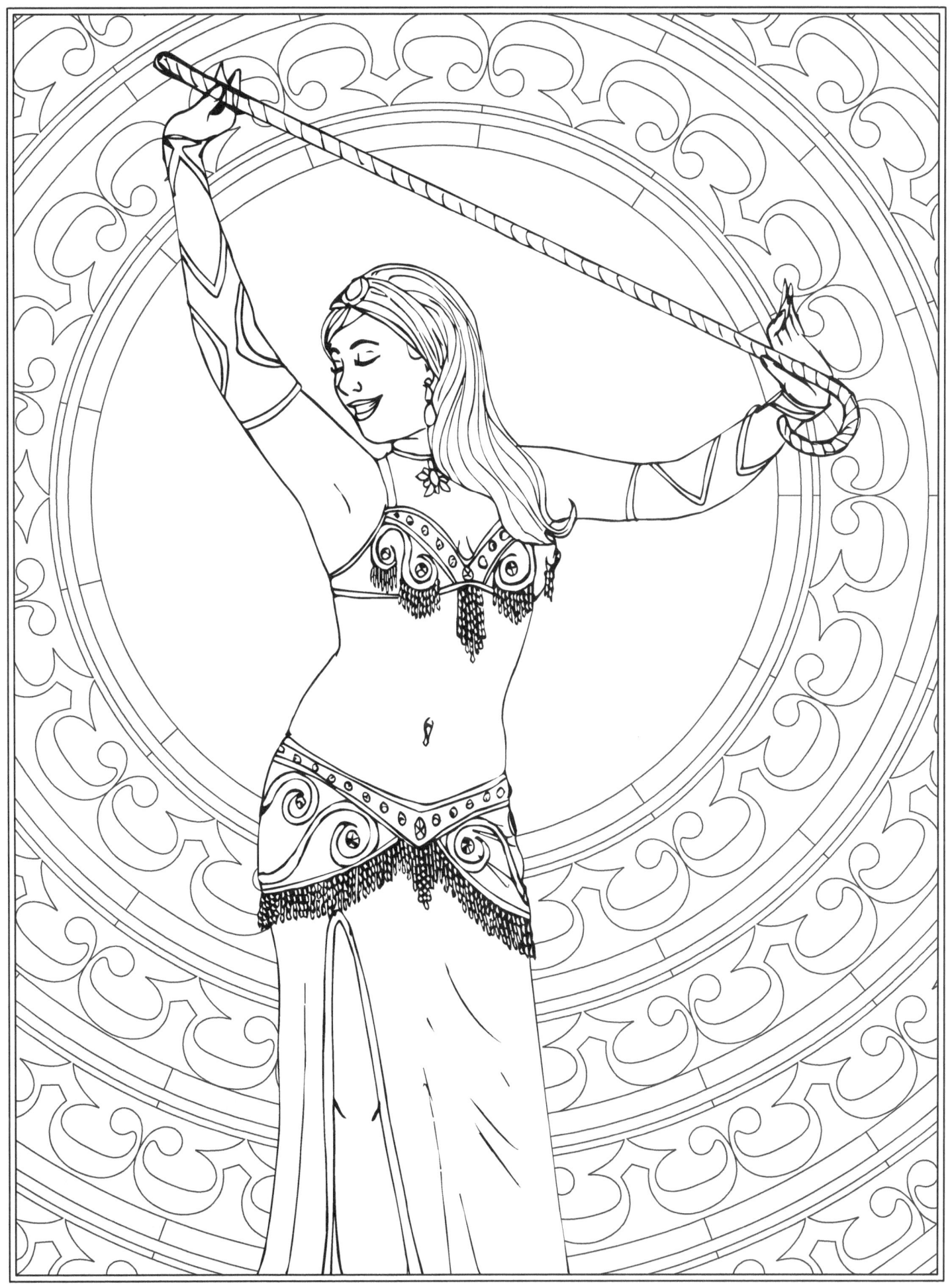

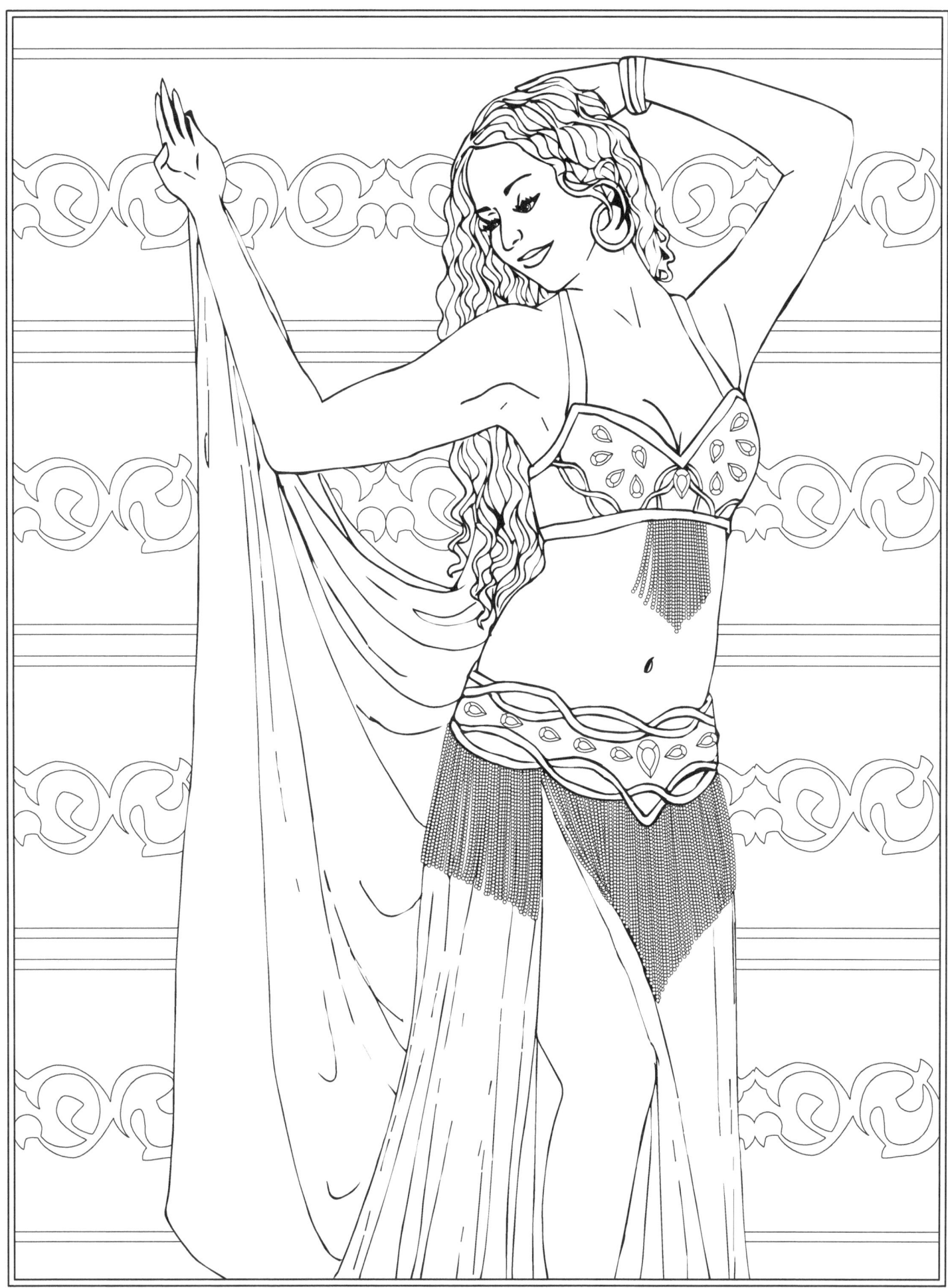

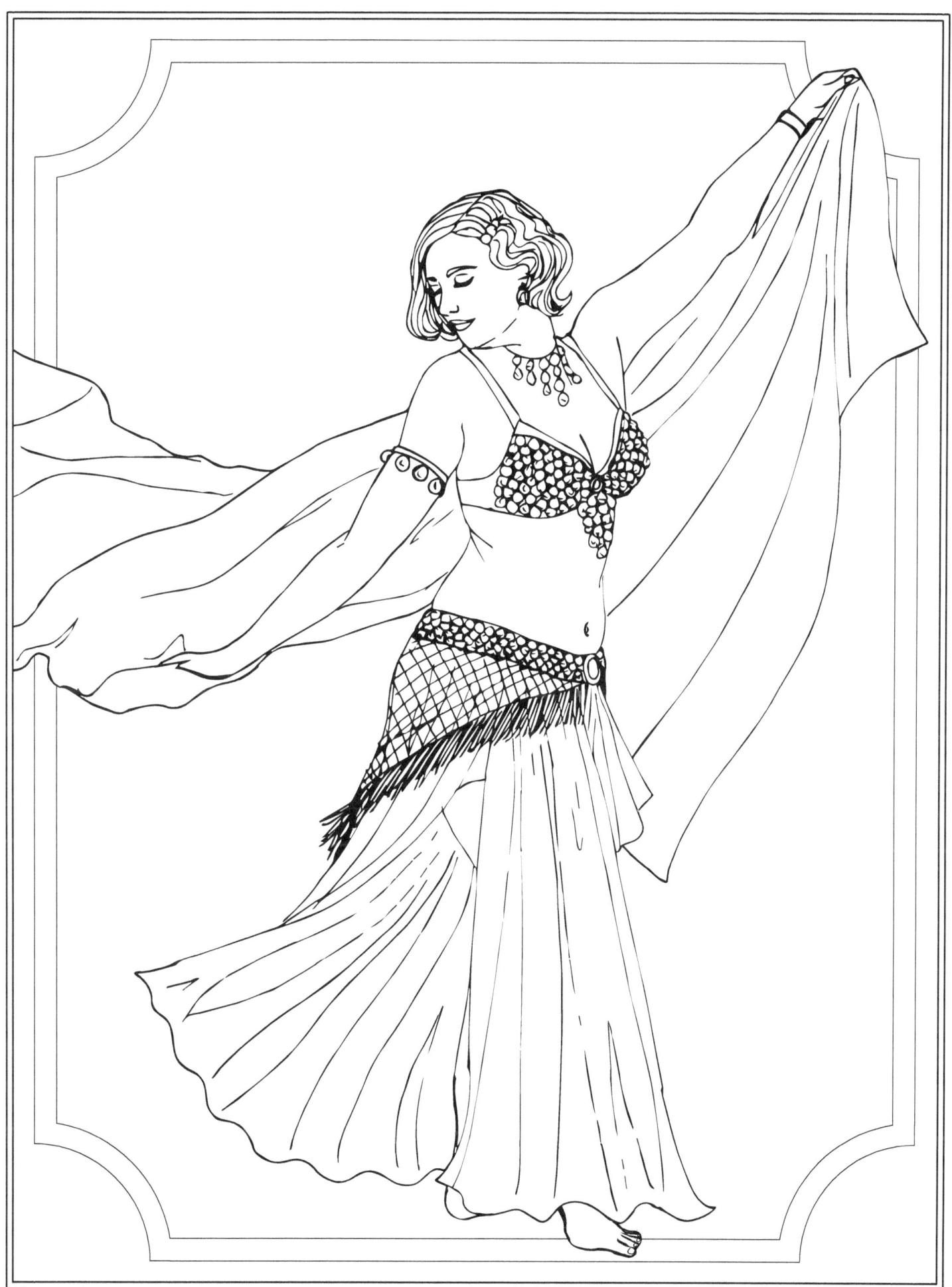

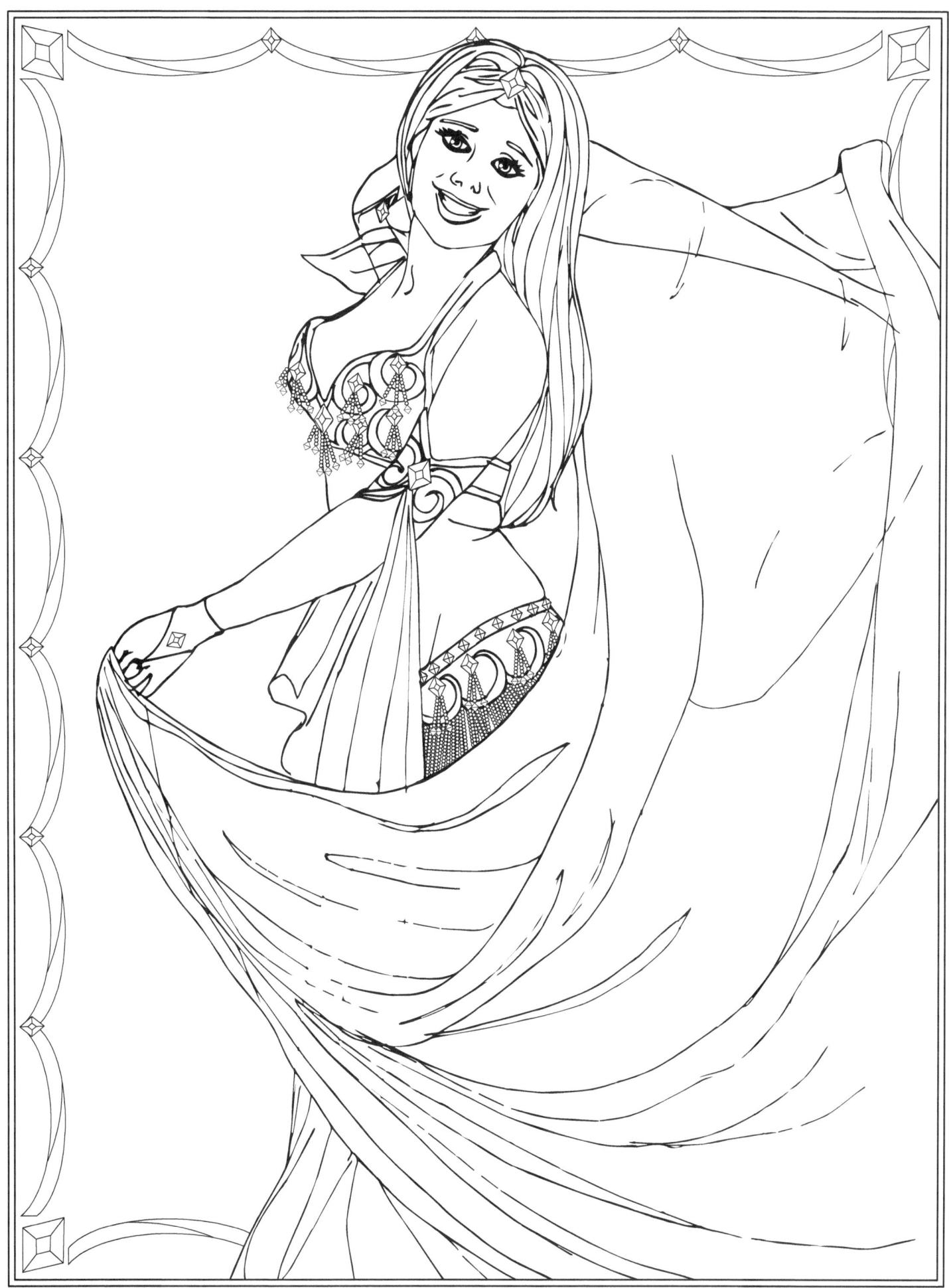

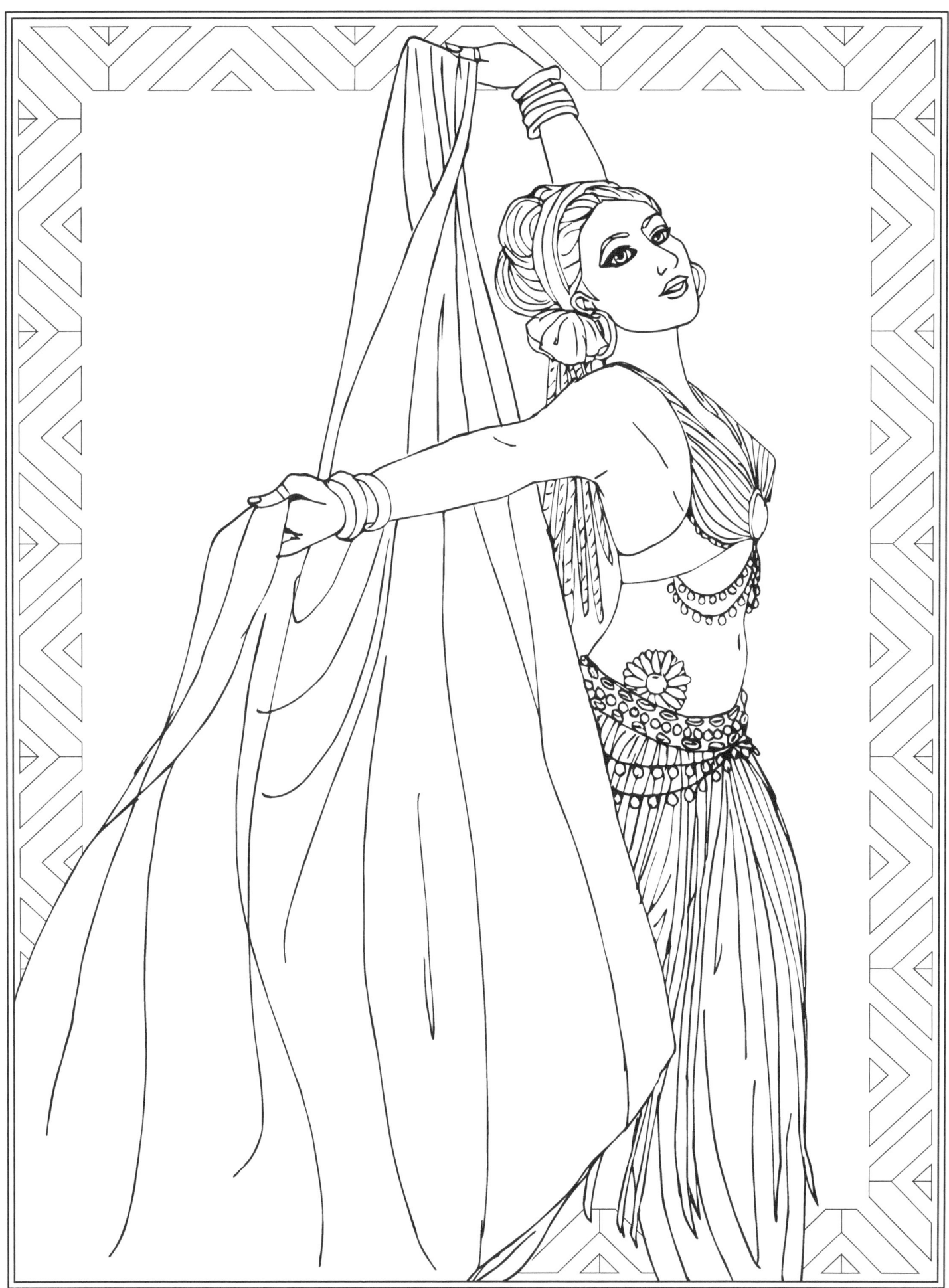

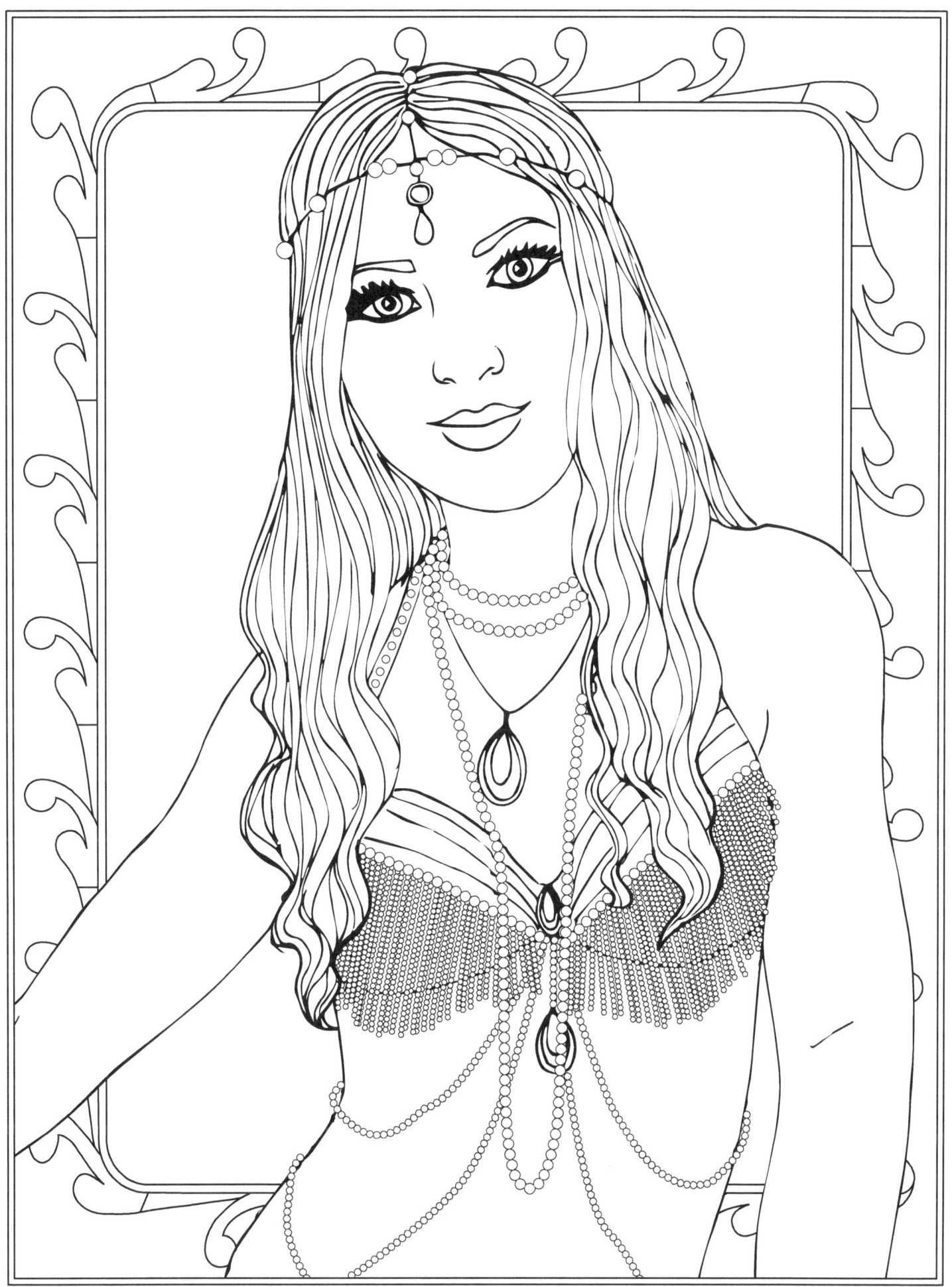

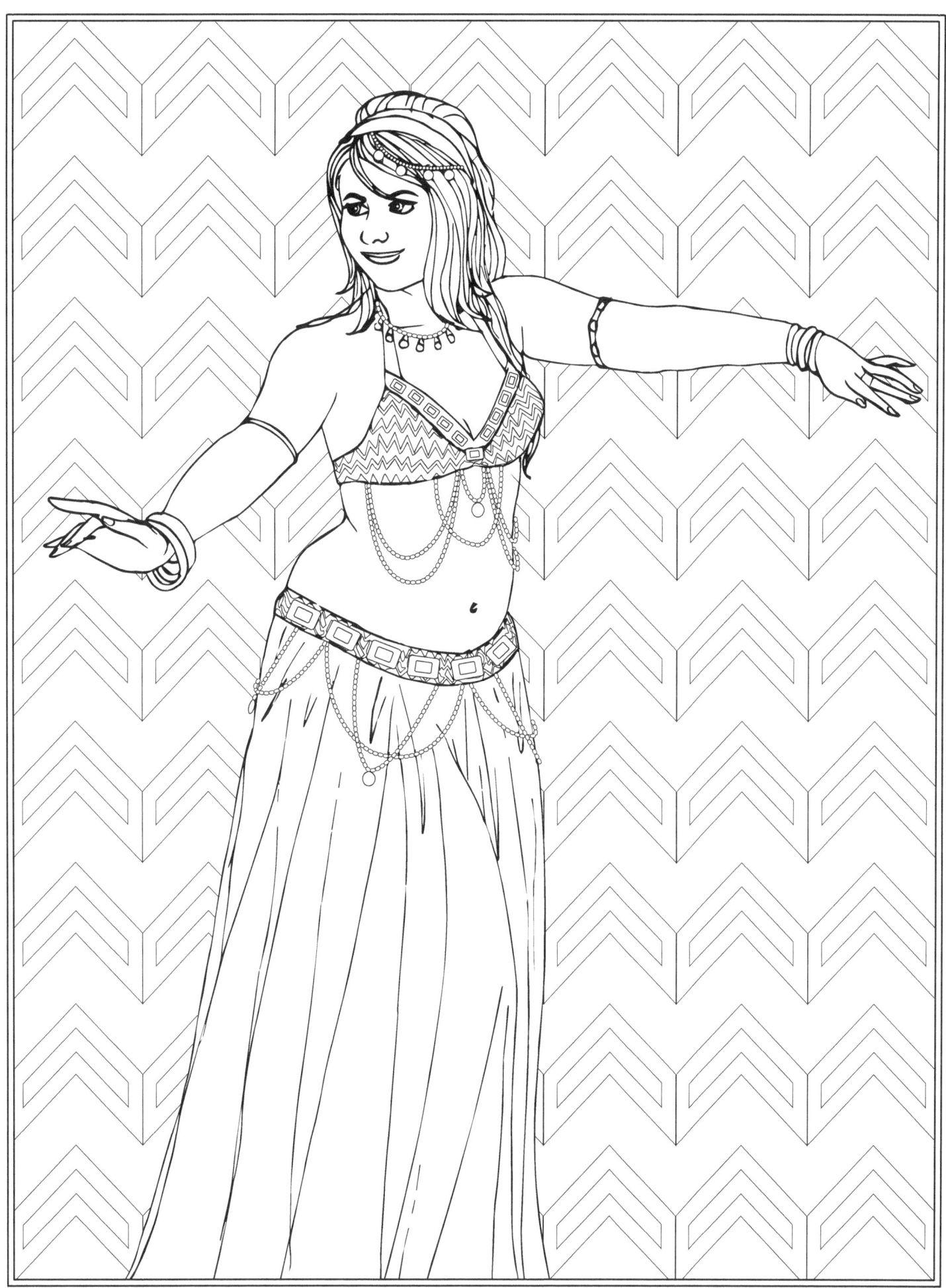

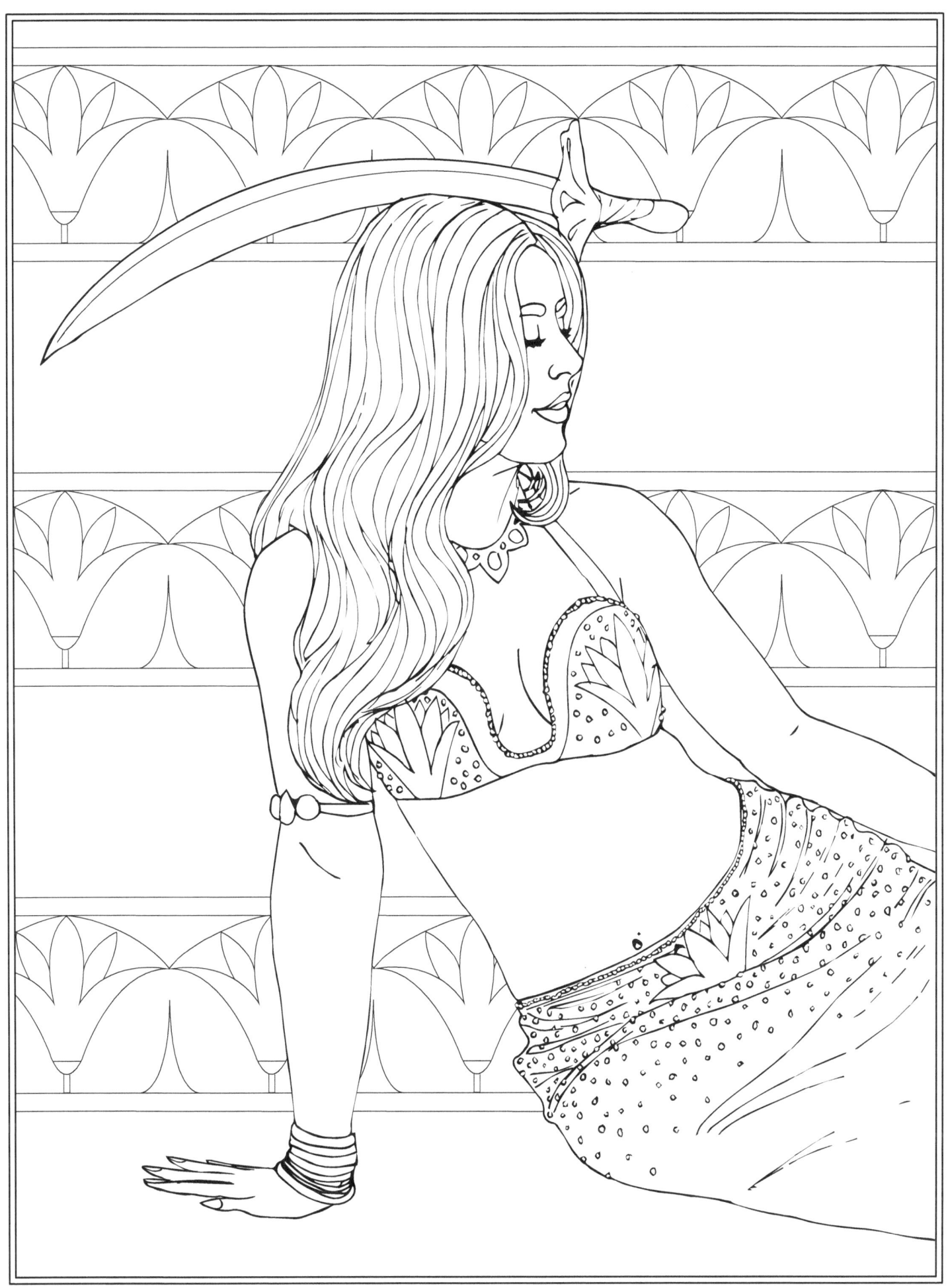

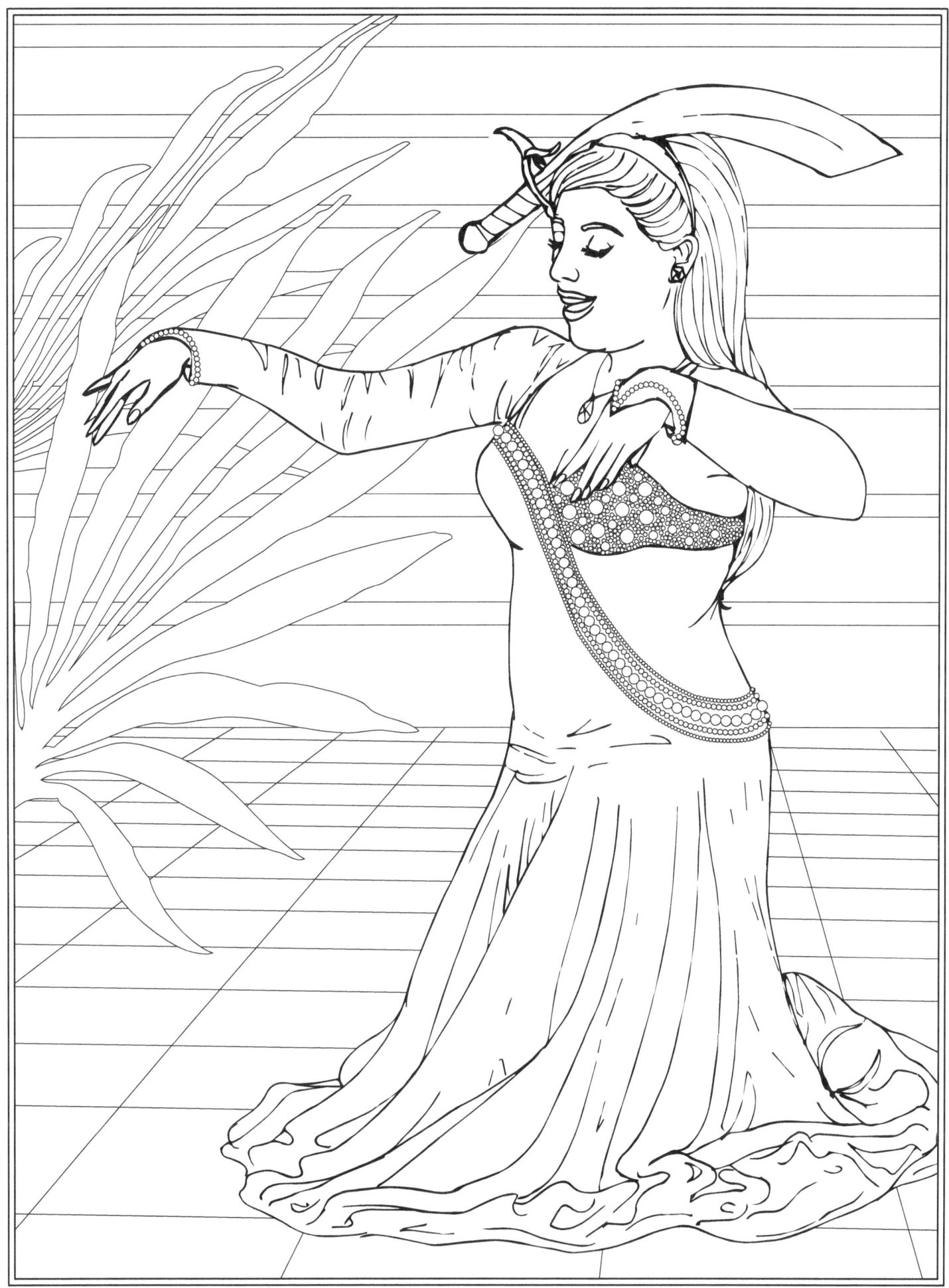

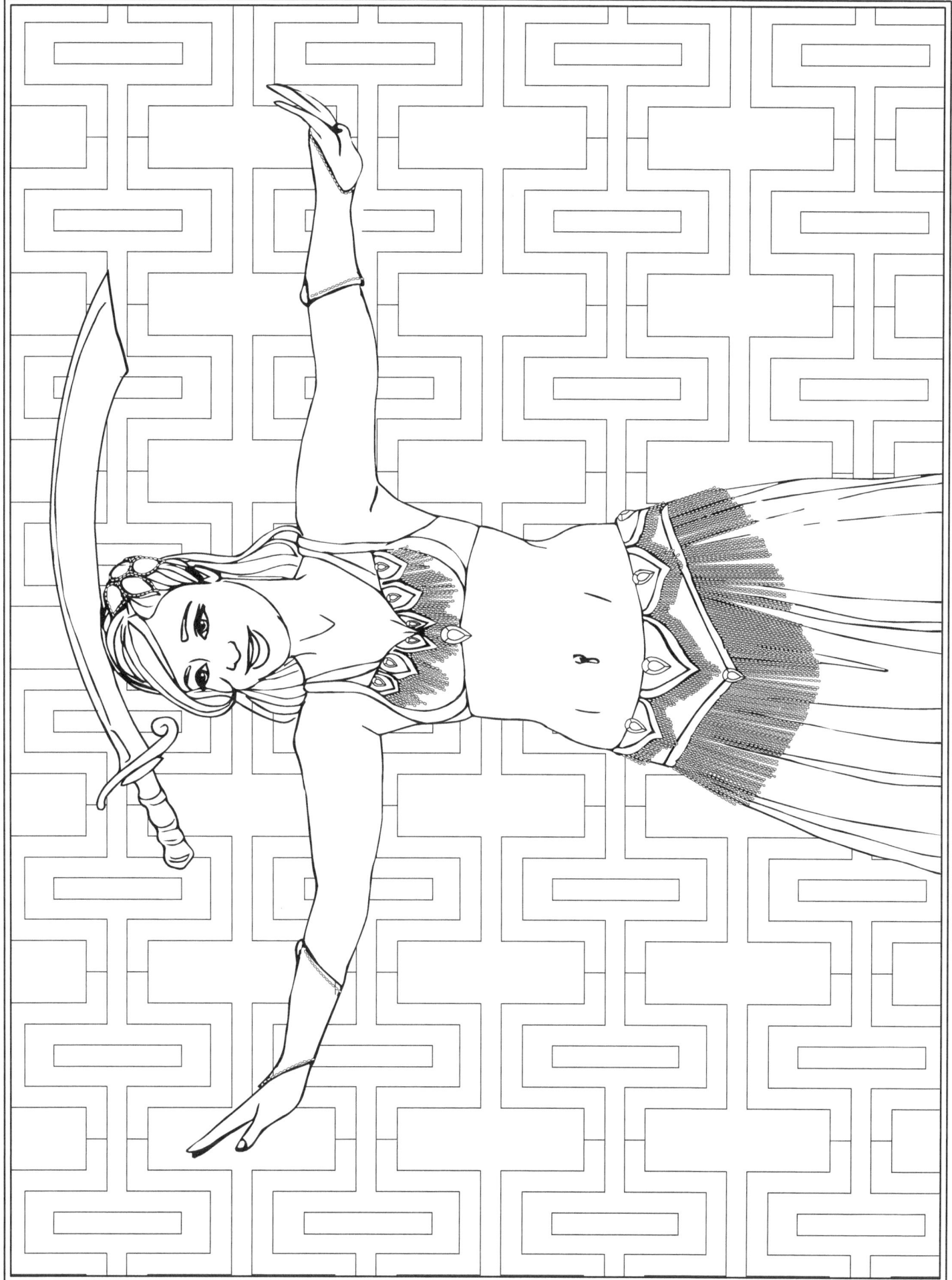

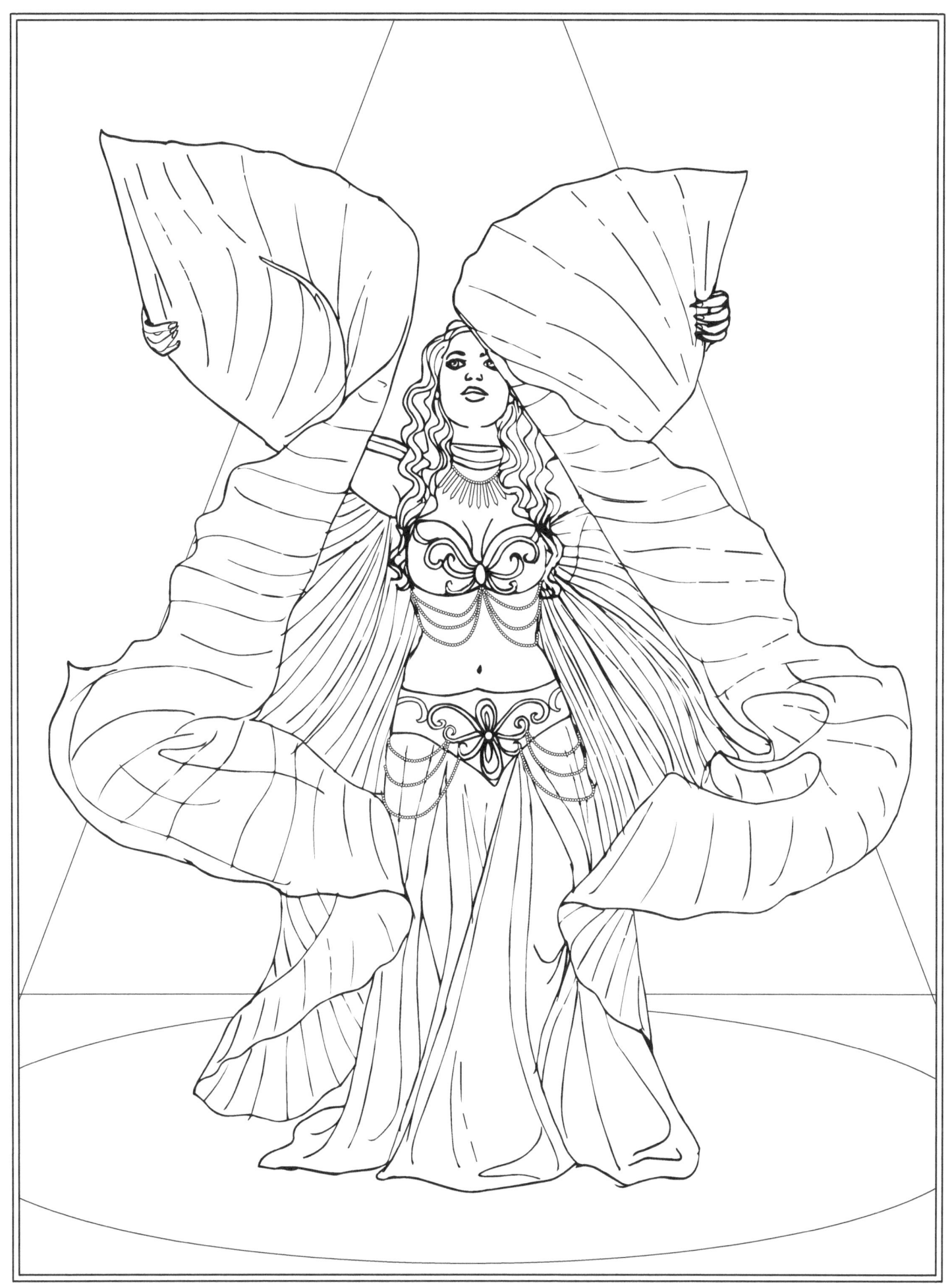

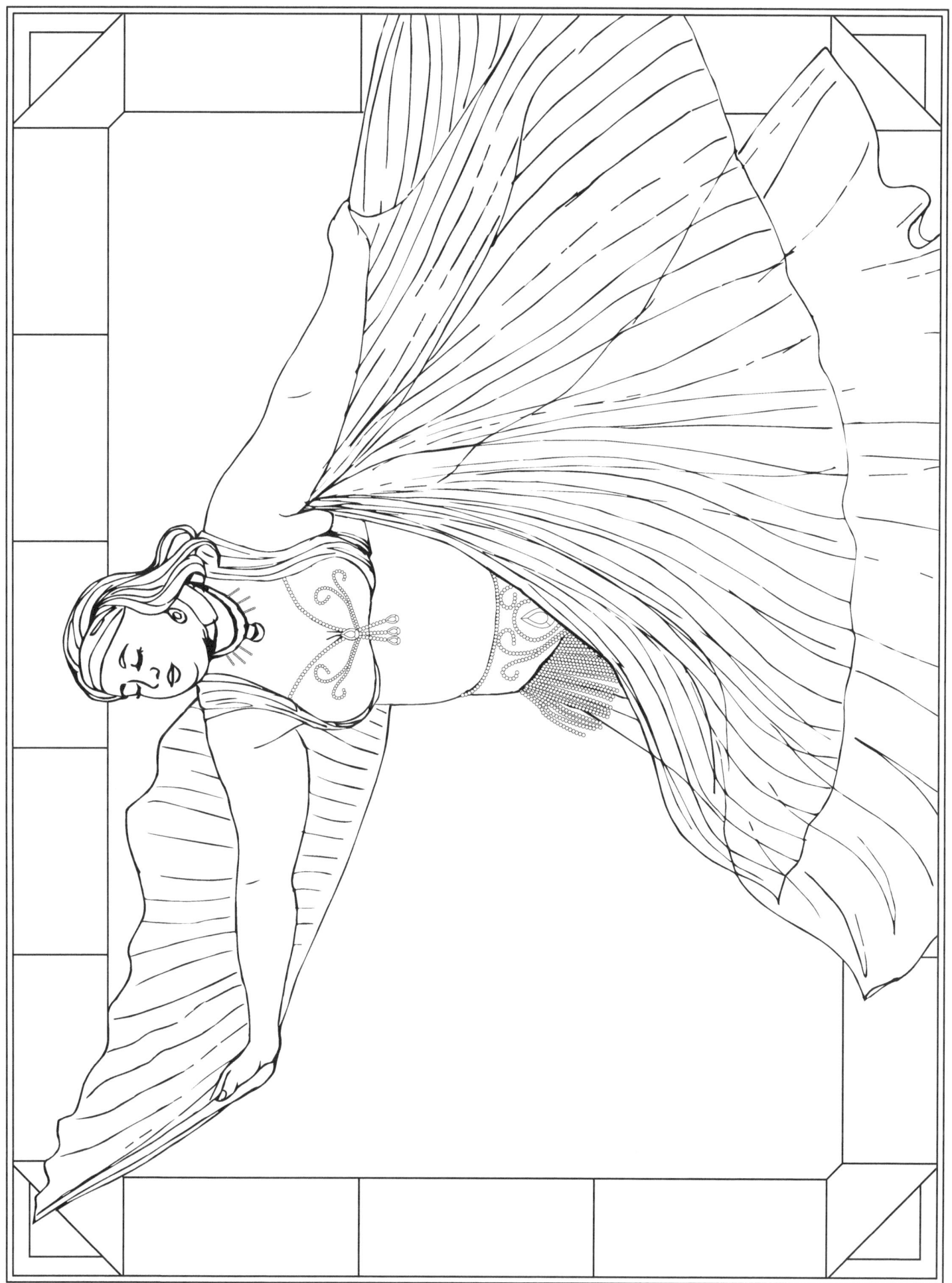

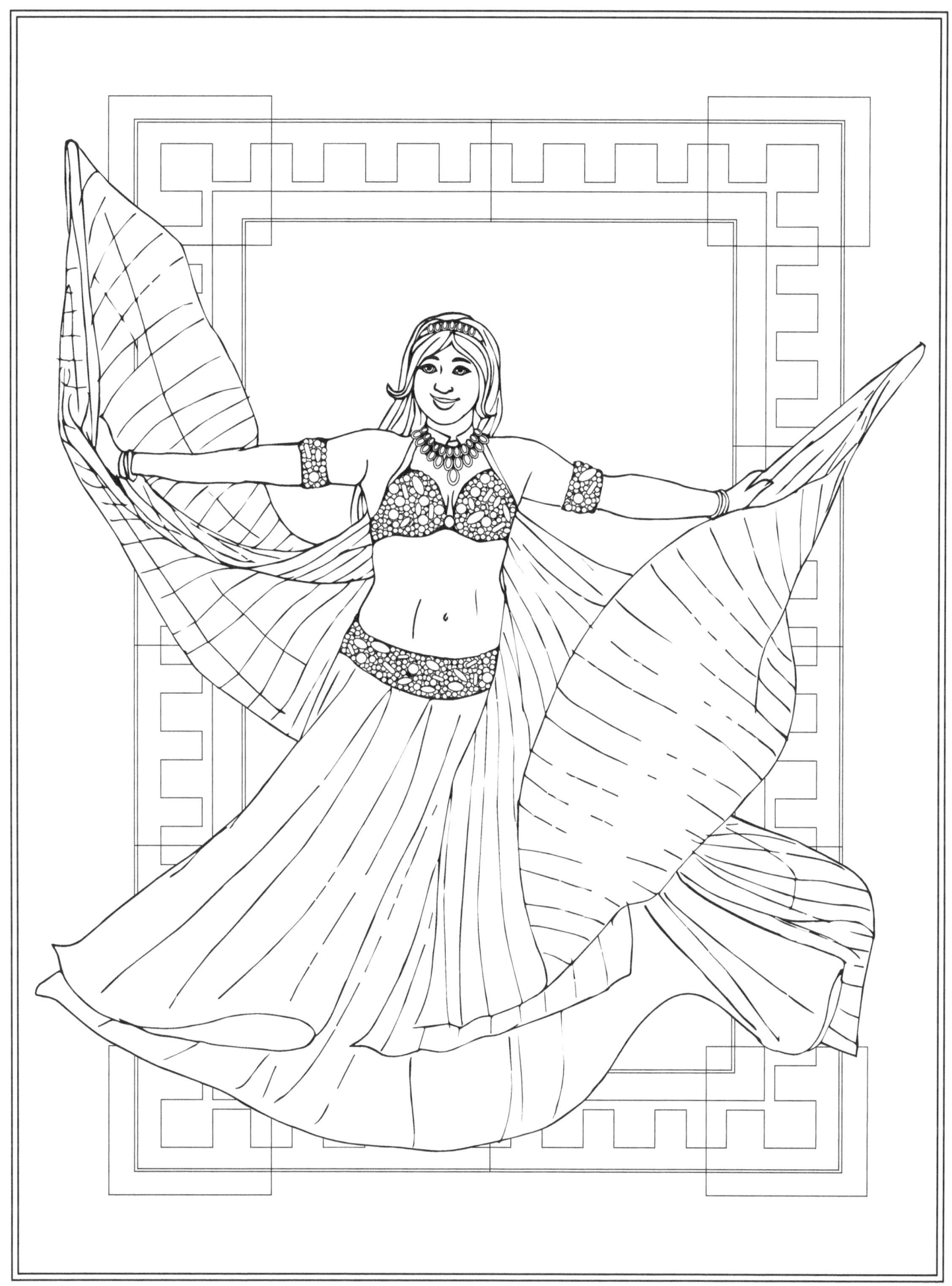

www.ingramcontent.com/pod-product-compliance
Lightning Source LLC
Chambersburg PA
CBHW081014170526
45158CB00010B/3032